Lessons from
a Writer's Life

Lessons from a Writer's Life

Readings and Resources for
Teachers and Students

Judith Ortiz Cofer

2011

HEINEMANN
Portsmouth, NH

Heinemann

361 Hanover Street

Portsmouth, NH 03801–3912

www.heinemann.com

Offices and agents throughout the world

Acknowledgments for borrowed material can be found on page 116.

Library of Congress Cataloging-in-Publication Data

Cofer, Judith Ortiz.

    Lessons from a writer's life : readings and resources for teachers and students / Judith Ortiz Cofer.

        p. cm.

    Includes bibliographical references.

    ISBN-13: 978-0-325-03146-0

    ISBN-10: 0-325-03146-0

    1. English language—Rhetoric—Study and teaching. 2. Creative writing—Study and teaching. 3. Authorship.   I. Title.

PE1404.C573 2011

808'.042'071'5—dc22   2010049805

Editor: Margaret LaRaia

Production: Vicki Kasabian

Interior and cover designs: Lisa A. Fowler

Author photograph: Steve Sortino

Typesetter: Kim Arney

Manufacturing: Steve Bernier

Printed in the United States of America on acid-free paper

15 14 13 12 11 VP 1 2 3 4 5

With love and gratitude to my ideal readers,
Billie Bennett Franchini and Kathryn Locey, and as always,
to the best teacher I know, John Cofer.

Mil gracias also to my editor Margaret LaRaia for her valuable
contributions to this book and her dedication to this project.
My gratitude also to Vicki Kasabian and Lisa A. Fowler for
the magic touches they added to this book.

contents

what i know viii

one **writers begin in memory** 2

"Invisible Me" | "Finding a Voice: The Language of Survival"

"The Welcome Mat: A Prose Poem"

"Seeing in American"

"Who Is the Alien?"

two **writers begin in images, dreams, and poetry** 20

"Underwater" | "A Life Boat"

"But Tell It Slant: From Poetry to Prose and Back Again"

"It's Like This" | "Where You Need to Go"

"Los Sueños and Poetry" | "The Need for Poetry"

three **writers begin in the words of others** 36

"The Yielding World: Pen, Fountain, Feather"

"Living in Spanish" | "Word Hunger"

"My Mother's Gift" | "Traveling with Alice in Wonderland"

"First Class Back to the Summer of Love"

"We Become the Monkey Girl: A Prose Poem"

resources 69

the craft of writing and why it matters: an interview with judith ortiz cofer 70

judith ortiz cofer's writing tools for students and teachers 76

Become a camera. **76**
Explore the importance of place. **77**
Watch the movie of what happened. **79**
Examine your life as part of history. **80**
Become a reader. **81**
Use poetry as a tool of revision. **82**
Write about others to learn about yourself. **83**

how i use judith ortiz cofer's work in the classroom 87

Engaging with the Work of Judith Ortiz Cofer,
    by Harvey "Smokey" Daniels **87**
Helping Students See Themselves as Writers, by Carol Jago **98**
Read. Imagine. Write., by Penny Kittle **106**

also by judith ortiz cofer 114

acknowledgments **116**

what i know

I DREW FROM MY EXPERIENCES as a child growing up in my native Puerto Rico, and later in New Jersey and Georgia, to create a structure for the pieces in this book. Together they tell the story of my self-invention as an American writer and teacher. I invite you to become my fellow traveler on the journey and to benefit from the lessons I learned along the way.

LESSON 1: language is a means of survival

Early in my American life, I discovered the power of language to transform my reality, to shape my future. My reality then was intrinsically connected to Spanish and to my native culture, which was the small but familiar and safe world our parents could offer us within the confines of our home and the boundaries of our barrio.

When I began to master the English language, the language of our survival, I expanded my borders. I added new dimensions to my reality, new options to my future. Little by little I reinvented myself as a new American, one who could travel between languages and cultures, adding rather than subtracting from each, taking what I needed for self-empowerment. In order to speak for yourself, you have to learn the language of power. I am not speaking simply as a nonnative English speaker, one who learned the language of survival as a second language. Although this is what I started out being, I speak now as someone who learned that words are power. And the words you need are found not in the street or on TV, but in books and in classrooms; the vocabulary of success is acquired through a deliberate effort, even if you are already a speaker of English. Words have the power to transform you and give you the power to shape your life. The minute you open your mouth, you have introduced yourself.

For me, language and an education have been the passport into the life I dreamed of living, the life that even those closest to me could not imagine as possible for me to achieve. I was able to dream a big dream because I had the words to express my goals. I am not the leader of the free world, a rock star, or a millionaire, but I am the captain of my ship. I teach and I write, and this is what I want and love to do. This is what my father wanted to do. He would have made a wonderful teacher—he had the intelligence but not the mastery of this language of power that would make his dream a reality. A good vocabulary and an education will not guarantee you immediate success, riches, or fame, but it will give you the courage to go after your goals. As a person who is educated and can use language well, you will have attained:

- the courage to think for yourself, and to articulate your ideas

- the courage to argue for your plans and to convince others that you are intelligent and capable

- the courage to lead a richer life, one that involves the enjoyment of reading, the appreciation of music, of performance, and of art. Boredom is nothing but mind hunger, and mindless entertainment is nothing but junk food. Immediate gratification is a sugar high. The goals you reach through your individual efforts are soul food.

LESSON 2: imagination can help you invent the self you want to be in the world

You become who you think you are. Dr. Seuss, one of my favorite writers, the author of such classics as *Green Eggs and Ham*, *The Cat in the Hat*, and *How the Grinch Stole Christmas*, once said, "Be who you are and say what you feel, because those who mind don't matter and those who matter don't mind."

Besides possessing the language of your survival, I cannot emphasize enough the importance of imagination. I know because of the pivotal role it played in reinventing my life. Imagination is the uniquely human capacity to envision a future. When you fail to see yourself as a participant in the human story, you have given your life over to inertia or put your story into the mouths of others. But imagining yourself as all you can be is not enough. To be fully involved in a rich, fulfilling life, you have to be able to identify with others whose experiences you have not shared. You have to listen to their stories. This is how I became a writer. I learned to observe and to listen. When I sit down to write a poem or a story, it is not just my experiences I draw from; I think beyond myself and try to imagine someone else's joys and troubles; I try to become my fellow human being. By writing about the other, and reading about the other, you learn how to live in the whole world.

LESSON 3: you can find beauty in the world by looking through others' eyes

"The future belongs to those who believe in the beauty of their dreams," said the great Eleanor Roosevelt, a woman who believed herself powerful and then embodied it in a world that resisted the concept.

I have spent my life trying to share a vision of beauty, and the most important lesson I learned in my long journey toward this day is that people are wrong who say beauty is only in the eye of the beholder. No, there is a true beauty we can *all* see, but first we have to learn how to see it through one another's eyes.

I'd like to share a poem that I hope conveys my idea of an inclusive common ground. This poem is not an attempt to have my two cultures melt in a pot but, rather, to have them naturally meld—and come together organically.

"To Understand *El Azul*" could not have been written if I had not met my husband and fellow teacher, John Cofer, when we were both eighteen. I learned through him that it is possible, indeed necessary, to try to appreciate a landscape through the eyes of another. By his example, I began to see red clay not only as beautiful but as a yielding element, mysterious as the ocean depths. The Georgia earth can be plumbed for its history, in arrowheads and artifacts that can be used to make numerous useful things; it can feed you most abundantly; and if inclined to do so (which I am *not*) you can harvest worms for fishing.

This poem might not have also been written if I had not received a commission from the university where I teach to write one for the freshman convocation that year. The poem needed to celebrate the diversity of our student population in some way—and finding a way was *my* task. I had never written a poem by request and was in a panic. I did not know how to begin such an endeavor until I got help from the two people in my life who love their very different native lands with equal passion: my husband and my mother.

My mother is featured in many of my poems and stories. She is my favorite devil's advocate and joyful opponent. The summer of my commissioned poem I went to visit her in Puerto Rico, and she did the usual—sat across from me at the table watching me agonize over a way to convey truth and beauty from a multicultural perspective. She suggested we go for a ride to "*refrescar la vista*"—an idiomatic phrase that transliterated means roughly "to refresh your vision." How right she was. She took me to a hill where we could see the ocean meeting the sky. The many hues of blue transfixed me. *Ese azul*, I said, awestruck. *That blue. Mi cielo, mi mar,* she declared. *My sky, my sea*—to her, the most beautiful sight in the world.

I came back to our farm in Jefferson County with half the vision I needed for this work. It was a time between seasons in Georgia—cool mornings, warm days—and from our porch, John pointed out his favorite sight: the early morning mist rising over the pond, and the ghostly figure of our resident blue heron, a mysterious presence, who arrives at our small body of water to rest from his journeys, then flies off again, not to be seen again for months.

John's vision of beauty combined with my mother's gave rise to this poem, which voices what I believe about coming together in this interesting, diverse, and complicated world: that one has to learn to find beauty and recognize truth from the perspective of another; that beauty and truth are reciprocal propositions. This is what I know. It may not be all I need to know to live, but with luck I will have time to discover the rest.

To Understand *El Azul*

We dream in the language we all understand,
in the tongue that preceded alphabet and word.
Each time we claim beauty from the world,
we approximate its secret grammar, its silent
syntax; draw nearer to the Rosetta stone
for dismantling Babel.

If I say *el azul*, you may not see the color
of *mi cielo, mi mar*. Look once upon my sky,
my sea and you will know precisely
what *el azul* means to me.

Begin with this: the cool kiss
of a September morning in Georgia, the bell-shaped
currents of air changing in the sky, the sad ghosts
of smoke clinging to a cleared field, and the way
days will taste different in your mouth each week
of the season. *Sabado*: Saturday

is strawberry. *Martes*: Tuesday
is bitter chocolate to me.

Do you know what I mean?

Still, everything we dream circles back.
Imagine the bird that returns home every night
with news of a miraculous world just beyond
your private horizon. To understand its message
first you must decipher its dialect of distance,
its idiom of dance. Look for clues
in its arching descent, in the way it resists
gravity. Above all, you have to learn why
it aims each day

toward the boundless *azul*.

"Language is a means of survival."

one

writers begin in memory

Invisible Me

As a child, with th... ...a hard accent
still tripping my ... ...averted eyes,
when my hand ... ...ecause I did
have the answ... ...
she posed—... ...
... ...disappoin... The jeer
... ...of the ... exp...
... ...onto my skin.
... ...ocking call. And so...
...myself one with rid...
...he art of self-defini...
...as an oyster.

Invisible Me

As a child, with the pebbles of a hard accent
still tripping my tongue, the teacher's averted eyes,
when my hand went up as reflex—because I *did*
have the answer to the simple problem
she posed—erased me from the room.

On the playing field, I sought to disappear. The jeers,
when I could not follow the rules of the game, exposed me.
I felt the motley suit graft itself onto my skin
patch by patch, with every mocking call. And soon,
I learned to think myself one with the gym wall.

In time, I mastered the art of self-definition, learned
to think of my mouth as an oyster,
making words out of irritation, pearls from sand,
and I drew and shaped myself, slowly
becoming visible to the ones who wanted to see.

Now I grant no one the terrible power
to make me nothing again.

finding a voice

the language of survival

AN INDIVIDUAL IDENTITY may be born out of choice, a dream for one's life may be created by making an active choice to live meaningfully. What is the alternative? Without mastery of the language of survival, without an education, life happens to you, with or without your permission.

I remember the misery of my first days in school before I spoke enough English to be an active participant in the classroom. I was small to begin with, but I tried to shrink into my desk at the back of the class, so as to avoid any possible eye contact with the teacher. I was not ready to engage in a conversation that would reveal my vulnerability. I felt defenseless and word hungry. For months, I managed to make myself invisible by being silent, but I also made myself sick. Sick with fear and anxiety. No words, no identity. Invisibility is not a normal condition, especially for a child. It means that you fear the same world you long to be a part of, and fear will eventually take over your life. Invisibility could become a chronic condition, as it has for people who remain trapped outside of language and end up avoiding the dangers and opportunities of the mainstream world.

Before I had mastered English, I was two people at the same time: the silent, unseen girl in the back of the class, and then, when I came home, my family's spokesperson and interpreter. My mother was fearless in Spanish, but inhibited in English. She claimed that when she spoke in English, her thick accent and hesitations made her sound ignorant, so she had me speak for her.

It was usually the landlord of our apartment building or the cashier at the supermarket for whom I had to translate my mother's words, and she demanded accuracy. "Did you tell him exactly what I said, Hija?" My basic vocabulary was good enough to get us through our daily struggles. But it was a national crisis that transformed me into an English speaker.

My poem "A Theory of Chaos" dramatizes what happened to me on that day in October 1962, the day when language became a matter of survival. My father was in the U.S. Navy and away on a dangerous mission. His ship was part of the embargo President Kennedy had imposed on Cuba during the missile crisis. We had not heard from him in months. At my mother's request I had been calling the Red Cross and the Navy office at Brooklyn Yard, my father's home base. I had experienced the humiliation of having adults patronize me, a ten-year-old with little English, asking questions she could hardly phrase.

"Tell your mother to call us if she stops getting her check every month. Otherwise, wait to hear from the government," I remember someone saying to me, speaking slow and loud, as if I were stupid or hard of hearing. "Tell her that unless someone comes to her door to tell her the bad news, she can assume your father is alive." I wrote these things down so I would not make any mistakes in my translations. But my mother would not accept these vague, harsh words as an answer, and I'd have to call again. I have never forgotten the powerlessness and guilt I felt when she'd break down in tears at the nonanswers I had to deliver. "*No puede ser*," she'd say, "This cannot be." Trust was what was lost in translation for her. Even at that age, I knew I had to possess English before it defeated us.

Then my mother got sick. It may have been the stress of not knowing my father's whereabouts, or of living in a bubble of silence without her extended family who were all back in Puerto Rico, at a time when a long-distance call, especially one that was considered international, was reserved, like telegrams, for times of extreme crisis or death. She could not just call her *Mamá* or any of her seven siblings for comforting words and advice. She had two little children, my brother and me. As the older child, I bore the burden of her anxieties, and my father had charged me with being her translator and the public face of our family. This was a lot of responsibility for a ten-year-old, but now I know that it was not, and still is not, my story alone. There are many boys and girls out there, children of immigrant families, who must internalize English not just to pass their classes but for the survival of their families.

My mother's fever peaked and she had me call a doctor we had seen before. I explained as well as I could that we had no transportation to go to his office and that my mother was too sick to take a bus. He agreed to call in some medicines to the nearest drugstore to our block. His nurse spelled the difficult names for me, and I wrote them in my notebook.

When I hung up, I was trembling. I had never left our barrio alone, except to walk to school, always in my mother's firm grasp. I could not pronounce the words in my notebook. I told my mother that I could not do it. I could not speak English. But she said, "I know you can do this, Hija. I will say a prayer to our Angel de la Guarda. He will accompany you."

Something happened to me that day on my way to get help for my sick mother. I was afraid yet completely focused on my mission. I started practicing words that I didn't even know I had in my brain and putting sentences together. I heard myself speaking these words in English. In my poem, written decades later, I try to articulate the mystery of language acquisition:

> My life was chaos
> shaped by chance, biology,
> and either *el destino*
> or circumstance. I did not know
> or care then
> that I carried the coded message
> to make language from pure need.
>
> But then,
> as I entered the too-bright drugstore
> alien as a space ship, sudden
> as Ezekiel's wheel,
> mysterious as the Annunciation—

© 2011 by Judith Ortiz Cofer, from *Lessons from a Writer's Life*. Portsmouth, NH: Heinemann. For full-page reproduction, photocopy at 118%.

I could understand the speech of people,

I could read the labels,

and raised my head up

to hear the voice

over the loudspeaker.

All was clear,

and fell into place . . .

I now know that what had happened was a natural process. For
months I had been subconsciously absorbing English, preparing to put
sounds into words and words into sentences, just as babies do. Then the
crisis of my father's absence and my mother's illness focused my need for
language. I could speak because I needed to speak, and also because I was
ready to speak my language of survival.

the welcome mat

a prose poem

SHE CAN WALK TEN BLOCKS, past the stores named after saints and pueblos, the church with the sign of a Pentecostal service *en español*, and the bar with a door that is always half open, where the sign for go-go girls—a strobing blue nude—is on day and night, past the buildings with slush piled up to the curb, with muddy paths stomped out by those who must slog through to cross the street; past where almost everyone she knows lives—ten blocks to a different world. The doctor's daughter, who wrote an essay for Sister Olive's English class about the goodness-grace of having friends of all colors and persuasions, has given her directions to her house, where they will do homework together. It is Lent, and she suspects the doctor's daughter is using her as currency against her venial sins. She will walk ten blocks beyond her gray world, walk until there is space and light, until the snow serves for decoration and play. A grinning-silly snowman in the yard. This section of town turns her into a wary-scary stranger, and she walks like one. The looks she gets from the cop watching over the neat houses and snow-plowed streets, and from the postman delivering something fragile right into a woman's hands at her own door, tell her to walk with purpose, eyes forward. It has snowed and she is wearing the wrong shoes. Chinese slippers made of fake suede that lets everything she steps on seep in. Her feet are numb by the time she arrives at the house with the circular drive. She leaves wet footprints all the way to the front door. There she is asked by the worried-smiling woman to please take off her shoes at the welcome mat before she steps onto the white shag carpet. White shag from wall to wall. What she remembers of this day is how her shoes curl up as they dry in the sun, like black clams, like two curly-dead creatures left on the welcome mat by the dog, and how her friend stares in silence at her little brother, who lets out a whooping–mocking laughlike sound when he sees her *zapatos muertos*. He whoops and jumps up and down once, before he covers his mouth and runs to the kitchen to share his dead shoes joke with his smiling-frowning mother.

Seeing in American

Our house was not your house, and our family was not
like your family. In old Kodachrome pictures,
where colors bleed, but are true to my dreams
and memories, I can now see the stark contrast
between our former selves and who we wanted to be.

Just look at our first American place,
with the Sears-on-credit furniture, its Armstrong
discontinued-pattern linoleum floors, patchworked
from room to room, the hard green sofa
and orange armchair covered in the cloudy plastic
the salesman had insisted anyone who was anyone
owned. We did not know how far off we were
from surmounting the color, shape, and pattern barriers
that separated *mi casa* from *su casa*.

How could we know
the heavy crucifix my grandmother sent us
to protect our home from malevolent influences,
hanging in the living room over the TV, where we watched
Mr. and Mrs. Cleaver living perfect lives in black and white,
did not repel, but drew the Evil Eye
from our rare outside-the-barrio visitors,
or that the vibrant, practically pulsating painting

of the Sacred Heart was inappropriate in the kitchen?
No one told us we would have to learn to think and dream
in pastel hues for years before we could see
in American.

who is the alien?

IN HIGH SCHOOL I WATCHED the TV show *Star Trek* and dreamed of a world where all my teachers looked like Captain Kirk of the Starship Enterprise and my parents acted logically and responded to my questions and demands in the measured tones of the second-in-command, Mr. Spock, who happened to be half human, half Vulcan, but mostly perfect. I dreamed of living in a world where all colors and races were represented as they were on the bridge of that ship: gorgeous and smart Lieutenant Uhura, cute Mr. Chekhov, the dutiful Mr. Sulu, the empathetic Dr. "Bones" McCoy, and the resourceful Scotty, who would beam me up out of any mess.

I watched the *Star Trek* episodes and then made up my own story lines, ones in which I substituted the heroes in *Star Trek* for the imperfect people in my real life. In my fantasy, my parents became soft-spoken Vulcans who would actually say things like, "It is only logical to allow our daughter to go out with her friends, as she is an intelligent, trustworthy person," instead of my mother's usual barrage of questions when I asked for permission to attend a party at one of my friends' or a school dance. In my mind I substituted my father's interrogations with a Vulcan mind meld. He would finally know without a doubt that I was not going to run away from home the minute he stopped monitoring my every move, and he would see that I had some reasonable plans in my head.

The mind meld did not happen, of course, but I did learn some things about logical thinking from Mr. Spock. I practiced raising one eyebrow in disdain for other people's faulty reasoning, and the hand sign for live long and prosper became my signature ending of a discussion or argument, which was a vast improvement over my bad-mouthing, door slamming *¡Adios!* that usually resulted in threats of being sent to a convent deep in the mountains of a *campo* on the island, where all the families I knew claimed to have a relative buried alive. I never found evidence of this medieval punishment; it must have been a threat that worked for Catholic families over the centuries. It certainly gave me nightmares that included imprisonment in a tower and layers of itchy clothing.

I also learned how to beam myself up, thank you, Scottie, out of the long, lonely days when we moved back and forth between Puerto Rico and the United States and I had to start over, making new friends and learning the ways of new teachers at new schools. I assigned each person a role on the ship that was my life: you are the captain (for now), to each teacher; you are the engineer or the space doctor (anyone on whose good sense I depended in a given situation: my driver's ed teacher, my dentist, my doctors); you are the leader of the Away Team (whoever became my guide and friend); and you, you are the unknown blue creature who may or may not be evil—I will keep my phaser on "stun" when you are around. I gave myself the directive to explore each new "world" cautiously, but with the determination of the one who is there to "seek out new civilizations . . . to boldly go. . . ." I was not always successful in my fantasy, of course. There were times when I was singled out as the alien, the odd one with the wrong-color skin and strange ways, and I felt stunned and shunned.

I was the alien in my new school in Augusta, Georgia, when we moved south in the late 1960s. It was a turbulent time of race tensions, and I entered a world as strange to me as some of the planets visited by the Star Trek crew. Even the landscape baffled me with its red earth. Everything about me, my black hair, my dark complexion, my New Jersey–accented speech, and my Spanish-speaking parents, set me apart in a culture that was much more homogenous than the multiethnic barrios I had known in New Jersey. In Georgia, I learned to empathize with the creatures in *Star Trek* who always had to prove their intentions were good, if they were. Understanding the alien's point of view gave me an advantage: I knew I had to study the mainstream group, and eventually decide whether I could be a part of it. It was not merely a matter of externals—I had to learn their ways if I was to survive in the place I had landed. I learned to listen.

My first and best friend that first lonely year in Georgia was a girl different from anyone I had ever known. She had translucent porcelain skin and green eyes. I never knew what her real hair color was, as she changed it from red to platinum and, after she decided she liked my hair, to blue-black in a matter of months. I was attracted to her because she waited for the bell to ring at the beginning of the day in the place I wanted for myself—the extreme far corner of the commons, against the wall, in no one's way. From that spot, away from the groups that congregated in cliques according to their levels of popularity, I could watch the action and take mental notes.

Arlene was tall and thin, long-legged, and, I thought, beautiful. But she hunched her shoulders and seemed to want to blend and disappear into the institutional green walls. The first thing I noticed about her was that she kept her eyes down. After watching her for a few days, I slunk over to her side. I was very curious as to why a girl who looked like she did acted as if she wanted to be invisible—although I was familiar with that urge myself. When you look different, sound different, and are looked at as if you don't belong, the only thing to do is to not call attention to yourself—the wrong kind of attention, even a simple question like *where are you from?*, can be painful to the outsider, especially a self-conscious teenager.

I don't know who said hi first; in her case, it would have been a Southern-drawled *hey*. But by lunchtime Arlene and I were Mutt-and-Jeff inseparable. I was tiny, with wild black hair to my waist, and she was statuesque with straight red hair (that month). By the end of the day I knew that she had three younger siblings and they all lived with their father, who was a self-employed electrician. She had to take an early bus home so she could be there when her little brothers and sister came home from school. Her mother had left them a couple of years ago, reasons left unspoken, whereabouts unknown, and Arlene was now in charge of the children and house. I could not imagine it, but I tried. In my mind I saw Arlene in a large, beautiful home greeting three lovely children who would look like her: porcelain dolls with green eyes. Her father would look and sound like Scotty. A problem solver. An ideal situation—a teenager under little supervision!

At fifteen, I was living in radically different circumstances, not in the least in charge of my environment or even of much of my life. My parents, although affectionate to a Latino extreme, were Puerto Rican–level overprotective, meaning that everything and everyone outside of the family and small circle of friends was suspect. And moving to Georgia had made my mother feel that all she knew and loved had been taken away from her: the Spanish-speaking neighbors, the barrio with its familiar business establishments, church services in her own language, and most of the social activities with other Puerto Rican people—the things that made her life in exile bearable, all gone. The only ones we knew in Augusta were my father's brothers, who were stationed in the Fort Gordon Army Post, and my aunts and cousins. We were not a community: we were a tiny enclave.

In time, all this would change dramatically as we made Georgia our home and re-created our lives, but the first few years we were like exiles in a foreign country. I needed a close friend, and when Arlene asked me to spend the night at her house, I argued for days with my parents until they relented. From Arlene's idealized home, I planned to bring back an arsenal of examples of the good life, American style, which I could use to reshape our lives. I also saw the visit as a chance to observe Arlene: I wanted to understand why she did not seem to fit in at school. I knew why I didn't—I was obviously an outsider—but she had it all. I even held a slight suspicion that just maybe she felt sorry for me and that is why she had befriended me, the alienated stranger at a school where the beautiful white girls (like her) could choose their friends among the elite and ignore the losers (like me).

A few months after meeting Arlene and hanging out with her in our favorite disappearing corner at school, of sharing gummy canned vegetables, limp lasagna, and, too often, shepherd's stew in the cafeteria and exchanging complaints about teachers and stuck-up girls who managed to look down at her even when she towered over them and didn't seem to see me at all, I began to wonder if it was because of me that no one offered to sit with us. Maybe Arlene was too kind for her own good. Yet I was happy enough to have one friend, and tried justifying our alienation as a result of her shyness; as for me, no need to look for reasons—I was used to being left out.

Arlene and I had interests in common—we both loved reading and watching TV, and we couldn't wait to get out of the limbo of high school and on to college. We sometimes talked about *Star Trek* and Arlene told me that she too fantasized about space travel. "That'd be one way to get away from it all!" Her favorite character was the doctor. "Hope I can work for someone that nice someday." She saw herself as a pediatric nurse in a hospital. "Taking care of pretty little babies all day for a living. What's better than that?"

My parents said no to Arlene's invitation until I argued them down point by point, logic against paranoia, my final weapon—inducing guilt; I would never adjust, always be unhappy, never forgive them for bringing me to Georgia (of all places!) unless they allowed me to have at least ONE friend.

I took the bus with Arlene after school and it dropped us off in a section on the outskirts of town I had not seen before. It was made up of small houses and even some cabins. Strangest of all, there were African Americans in their yards, on porches, and socializing on the sidewalks. It was an unusual sight because, in the late sixties, a city like Augusta did not have many integrated neighborhoods; even the school I attended had only two black girls in a population of over one thousand students. The diversity of the barrios and multiracial society of New Jersey, where we had lived most of my life, was something my whole family missed, mainly for reasons of survival, not just political correctness: we were comfortable among multicultural, multiethnic people—we did not stand out. In the South there were two colors represented in the population, and the line between them was clearly drawn. But Arlene was walking on a street where there seemed to be a blurring or some kind of space warp that allowed a white family to live in the middle of a black neighborhood.

I noticed that she walked a little taller and that people smiled at her; they saw her. One older African American woman we passed gave her a hug and asked her about the children. She said she'd send some barbeque over tomorrow from the birthday party her daughter was giving her. "Drop by if you can," she nodded at me, including me in the invitation. Then she held Arlene's hands and asked in a low voice if they had enough to eat that night. Arlene said, "Yes, M'am, thank you." They hugged again and we walked to the end of the block. We stopped in front of what I can now identify as a shotgun shack. It was a dilapidated little house, boxy, longer than wide, with a red tin roof. There was a junk-strewn yard, and a tan sofa that looked like a dead animal on the porch. I was stunned by the rancid smell that emanated from the interior when Arlene opened the door. Toys were strewn on the floor and she had to move clothes from a chair so I could sit down.

In her usual sweet voice Arlene said, "Sorry it's kind of messy. I don't have time to clean and the kids just mess things up again. Want some lemonade?" We were not alone more than a few minutes before a little girl about six and two boys who must have been under ten burst in and went straight to the refrigerator.

Arlene kissed each one, and went into a frenzy of activity washing glasses in the sink, pouring lemonade, and asking for a report of their school day. She tore open a package of cookies for them, and made the kids sit on the floor in front of an old TV to watch cartoons. She and I tried to talk above the noise of the kids squabbling and the Popeye show on TV. Mostly, I looked and listened as Arlene explained how she managed to keep "all those darn plates in the air" going to school and taking care of the kids. She made her story an amusing anecdote instead of a tragic tale. But I looked closely at Arlene's face and saw her sadness and her exhaustion. I listened to her voice and heard a little despair creep in beneath the funny phrases that sounded like a song with the lilt in her speech. I heard her not talking about her dire situation but instead about her plans to go to nursing school at the Medical College of Georgia when she graduated from high school. I noticed that her clothes were old, and suddenly I realized that she wore the same sweater practically every day. Admiring her looks and her voice, and taken by her charm and easy affection, I had not noticed the signs of her poverty.

But even though I felt sympathy for Arlene, I also understood that I had been wrong about her "alienness" in comparison with mine. She was an integral part of the world in which I had landed, and I had committed an error in judgment in assuming that because she looked like the successful others she was naturally in a better place than me. After a few hours in her sad home, I longed for my orderly *casa* where my illogical but dependable parents worried over my well-being—a little too much, perhaps. Hearing one of the children say "I'm hungry" to their sister was not the same as coming home to my mother, who would be cooking the predictable Puerto Rican food, and declaring, "I'm hungry. Can't we have hamburgers for a change instead of rice and beans, again?" My hunger would be satisfied without the moment of panic I saw in Arlene's eyes as she dug through her purse for a few dollars to send her brothers out for McDonald's burgers, a treat because they had a guest that day.

That night, the kids went to bed in one room, and Arlene and I shared the smallest, lumpiest foldout bed I have ever slept on. I hugged the wall all night, waking up once when I heard her arguing with a man; her father had come home angry for some reason—I suspected it was her having a guest. I pretended to sleep through it.

The next day was Saturday. I had instant coffee with Arlene and she asked me to stay—she was planning to go to her neighbor's for the birthday celebration, and she knew I'd be welcome. She also gave me her bad news in the sweet, melodious tones I once thought meant cheerfulness instead of simply being a way some Southerners have of expressing acceptance or resignation: a kind of Deep South brand of existentialism. "Bless his heart, Daddy's got a new job. We'll be moving." Later I understood that any statement of even the most profound disappointment or outrage may begin with forgiveness for the perpetrator: *bless her heart, she left her children;* or *bless his heart, he ruined my life.* That day Arlene told me that her father had accepted a job in another city as if she were merely announcing a vacation.

"When?" I felt both fear and hope for my friend. How could things get worse for her? She might find some relief if her father brought home more money, if she could concentrate more on her books than on child care and sheer survival. I also felt sorry for myself—so far, Arlene was the only person with whom I'd connected. I didn't want to lose her.

"Bless his heart, Daddy doesn't know when or even exactly where we're going. We've moved around a lot. He's just like that."

"What will you do?"

"Honey, I have to go with the kids. My little darlings don't have a mama now. I'm it."

One day that year, Arlene just stopped showing up to school. I asked about her, and was told that no one knew (nor cared—I heard the *neither* implied). "Bless her heart, Arlene's family is white trash. No accounting why they do anything." This statement contained the answer to what kind of alien Arlene was: it had nothing to do with what made us aliens. It wasn't skin color, language difference, or place of origin. She had simply been born to people who did not or could not follow the rules of their society, whether northern or southern, one that rejects the ones who stray beyond the boundaries of "normal" behavior. At school, Arlene had been put in her place and ignored: against the wall. She had been made invisible so she could not remind the more fortunate ones of what one or two degrees of separation can do to anyone's life.

Although I lost track of Arlene, I knew that she had at least two things in her favor: she was capable of loving her siblings enough to work toward her goals, and given the most minimal support and encouragement, she'd attain her dream of becoming a nurse. I still look for her face in hospitals and doctors' offices, and listen for her melodious voice. Arlene was also able to step lightly over race and color barriers, not in the usual way—the mainstream person coming to the aid of the other, that less fortunate person—but in reverse; she received the help she needed and the affection she craved, graciously, from people who were externally different, whose circumstances she shared, and whom she acknowledged as family. To me, these are the qualities of a survivor: to know how to give and to receive in equal measure.

By seeing myself in someone so apparently unlike me as Arlene, I completed the lesson I had begun to learn by watching and listening. I put my life in perspective: I was not the poorest, loneliest teenage girl I knew, and my parents having transplanted us from familiar New Jersey to foreign Georgia did not mean the end of the world. At least I had a home with two parents, and they provided, if not luxuries, the necessities, and a little more. I also saw that Arlene's survival depended on her trust and acceptance of others, and that is one of the lessons I did not learn from my parents, whose fear of the strange world outside the family group is a common one among immigrants. Not that I have completely shed my inclination toward suspicion and my guardedness, but I have learned to think of new places and new people as an opportunity to test my social skills.

It is easy to see what we saw in *Star Trek* and what most teenagers perceive—themselves as intrepid explorers. To boldly go, that is what Arlene and I had to learn how to do. If we chose not to dream, even as we lived our difficult lives, what was the alternative? Arlene chose a dignified serenity, a calm acceptance of her situation, taking care of her family to the best of her ability while still dreaming of a better world they could all inhabit—a pretty extraordinary accomplishment for a sixteen-year-old girl. I identified with her in spite of our cultural and physical differences because I saw that although she looked and sounded like the natives, she too was an alien in their midst. I aspired to reach her level of being. I wanted to be not the alien who remains alienated but the one who becomes a guide.

"Imagination can help you invent the self you want to be in the world."

two

writers begin in images, dreams, and poetry

underwater

I heard the art teacher say,

we will draw a cruz-ship today.

Children, we will all go on adve

on the ships of your imaginations.

Each on our own, with our crayo

and blank paper, we worked on

in our heads. I knew that cruz

and Julio behind me had said

with him

Underwater

I heard the art teacher say,
we will draw a cruz-ship today.
Children, we will all go on adventures
on the ships of your imaginations.

Each on our own, with our crayons
and blank paper, we worked on what we saw
in our heads. I knew that *cruz* means a cross
and Julio behind me had said *un bote*,
when I checked with him on variations for ship.

It was after recess, when we came back to a display
over the chalkboard in our classroom,
that I learned the meaning of shipwreck. Everyone
was pointing to the fisherman's dinghy
with a Spanish conquistador's cross on its sail,
my *bote* with a *cruz*.

I saw my little boat flounder in the wake
of my classmates' towering cruise ships.
The gales of their mocking laughter
swept me away in a violent current,
like so much seaweed,
to my place in the back of the room,
and the teacher's shouts of "Quiet! Sit down!
She doesn't understand—" pulled me down,
down, like tentacles, deep into my desk
and back to the familiar
underwater silence I understood.

a life boat

LIKE THE POET, the immigrant is primarily a metaphor maker, a translator of experience. Struggling between languages, I learned this skill early: how to answer the question *¿Como se dice?* by making a comparison, by trying to access the unfamiliar road by following the familiar *camino* first. When I heard an unfamiliar word, I went through my mental files for a comparison. In the poem "Underwater," I recall one of the "shipwreck" moments early in my American life: a day when a teacher innocently assumed that all her students knew what a *cruise ship* was. I did my best to guess what she wanted based on what I had experienced in my Spanish-speaking life. In Puerto Rico, I had seen the fishermen's dinghies in the seaside *pueblos* that we visited. I thought I heard the teacher say the word *cruz*, a familiar symbol in the Catholic church I attended and in my home. My parents and grandparents had books on Puerto Rico's Spanish colonial days, so I knew that some ships were adorned with crosses. I used all I had to come up with my "cruz-ship." My efforts were met with disdain by my fellow students, and the teacher's attempt to gain sympathy for me by reminding the class that "she doesn't understand" only made me feel more alienated.

These are the moments that are seared into the memory of a child struggling to master a new language: when you fail to know what everyone is supposed to know, and therefore to be "like everyone else." But something I understand now is that my story could have been interesting to the class if the assignment had been a bit more open. If we had been asked to draw our favorite boat, or one that we had seen. It could have been a time to share knowledge, an occasion for the others to see what I saw, rather than a setback in confidence for the student who "doesn't understand."

Recently I witnessed the empowering effects of giving a story to the students rather than simply dictating it. In a middle school classroom I visited in Atlanta, there was one Latino student, Alejandro, the silent one in the back of the room. His class had read some of the stories in my book *An Island Like You: Stories of the Barrio,* and their teacher had assigned them each to write and deliver a three-minute monologue based on their favorite character. It was exciting for me to hear how individual students transformed my characters into versions of themselves by giving them new voices, new mannerisms, and new ways of explaining their actions.

The teacher had warned me that Alejandro might not participate. He was, she said, aggressively silent, refusing to answer questions in class, and she feared that he was destined to drop out of school to follow his migrant worker parents as soon as he could. Alejandro did wait until the end of the presentations. He then walked to the podium and, standing very straight, delivered a monologue that left everyone stunned by its power. It was based on a character I created, who is in rebellion and close to losing everything, including his freedom. Everyone thinks he's a gangster because he is just plain bad, but in reality he is grieving for the mother he recently lost and is unable to help his father, who has also been defeated by emotional pain. In the story he finds love, and he also learns a lot about giving. Alejandro read his monologue in a thick Spanish accent, which was exactly right for the character. He read it dramatically, and with emotion. His resolve to make each word he said count brought tears to his teacher's (and my) eyes. I observed his fellow students looking at Alejandro with a mixture of wonder, curiosity, and maybe (I hoped) a growing sense of respect. Later, I saw that several girls came up to him at the reception we had at the end of my visit, and I saw that Alejandro was not being "aggressively silent" with them.

I do not know Alejandro's personal history, but I did hear from his teacher that she used special readings of material that she thought would draw him out in her class, and that he had become the Latino "expert," fielding questions about concepts and words that his fellow students would have had to look up. She had leveled the field, allowing him some time as the one who knows the answers, rather than the one who does not understand.

but tell it slant

from poetry to prose and back again

From poetry . . .

The Lesson of the Sugarcane

My mother opened her eyes wide
at the edge of the field
ready for cutting
"Take a deep breath,"
        she whispered,
"There is nothing as sweet:
Nada más dulce."
           Overhearing,
Father left the flat he was changing
in the road-warping sun,
and grabbing my arm, broke my sprint
toward a stalk:
"Cane can choke a little girl: snakes hide
where it grows over your head."

And he led us back to the crippled car
where we sweated out our penitence,

for having craved more sweetness

than we were allowed,

more sweetness than we could handle.

To story . . . from an early draft of *The Meaning of Consuelo*:

We often had tire blowouts and car trouble. Everyone did then, and so we knew the routine when we heard the familiar pop and Papi began to maneuver the car off the paved road. Since it was sweltering hot, Mami got out, looked around wherever we were to make sure it was safe, then she'd let me and Mili, my *prima-hermana*, my cousin who was living with us, come out for fresh air. She would take these occasions to point out things about our *país* to us as if we were *turistas*.

One day we had a flat by the side of a field of sugar cane that extended toward the horizon like a green sea. It was ready for harvesting. *La zafra*, the cutting season, is also the time of fiestas on the island, and we were heading for Mami's *pueblo* to the festival of the town's patron saint, San Lázaro. We would stay with her *Mamá* a few days and Papi would return to San Juan by himself since he had to go back to work.

Mami's happiness about going to her *mamá's* was evident in her movements, which were like a dancer's. In fact she had put on a mambo record to do her mopping the day before, and Mili and I had pranced around the house as she polished the floors while dancing with the mop to the sounds of Tito Puente and his orchestra.

Now her starched red cotton skirt and off-the-shoulder peasant blouse made her look like a movie star on vacation as she scanned the cane field, shading her eyes with one hand and holding both Mili's and my hands with the other. This was Papi's rule: if there was even the slightest possibility of a moving vehicle in our path we must be securely attached to an adult by the hand. I was beginning to resent this at the age of ten, but Mami only obeyed Papi's excessively protective commandments when he was around, so we had a silent agreement, she and I. We humored him in exchange for other privileges we exacted from each other. Mili had not yet caught on to these tactics, however; she seemed impervious to the family negotiations that went on constantly as we circled one another trying to figure out how to gain the most territory without starting a war.

"What are you looking for, Mami?" Mili asked, now six, pretty and vivacious as a Puerto Rican Shirley Temple with her mass of black curls, peach skin, and pearly white teeth. Mami could not help but hug and kiss her at least once an hour, by my rough calculations. I liked her too but I knew she had a bad side. In fact I had saved her from herself quite a few times. Mili was impulsive, even reckless. And I was always to blame for her mishaps, as her custodian by default since I was older. I was beginning to suspect even then that her "charming" personality would be her downfall.

"I'm trying to see if the cane is ready to eat," Mami whispered, bending down to look us in the eyes, "there is nothing sweeter than *la caña* of this part of our *isla, Hijas. Es pura azúcar.*" Then she crossed her lips for silence. I knew why she was speaking low. Papi did not allow us to eat anything that had not been "processed." That meant either it bore a seal from some U.S. government inspector or he had examined the product for worms, decay, pits, bones, or fibers that would choke his little girls; of course that meant depriving us of much of the island's bounty on which Mami had grown into the healthy woman he had married. "Country people learn early to deal with dangers you have not faced or will need to face," he had explained to me when I had been forbidden to suck on a *quenepa*, a slippery gooey fruit with a pit about the size of my gullet. One of my aunts had brought Mami a bunch from a tree in my *abuela's* yard. Papi's "No" had been firm enough to send me crying to my room. But when he left for work, Mami had brought in a few in a paper bag, then with deliberation she had shown me how to curl my tongue around the *pepita* so that it would not slide down my throat, and how to suck on the flesh of the fruit and savor it while rolling the pit back and forth in my mouth. It was a complicated but satisfying way to enjoy a forbidden fruit—absolutely worth the trouble and the price.

Mili suddenly broke loose from Mami's grasp and ran into the field. We both called out her name and my father dropped the tire he was about to mount on the wheel and ran after Mili. We watched him grab her by the arm a little too roughly and hurry her back to Mami.

Caught by surprise, Mili was not sure what she had done wrong as she ran to Mami. Papi looked sternly into Mami's face as he said to us, "There might be snakes in those stalks. Mami should be a little more careful about what she promises you."

He then opened the car doors and waited for us to get settled in seats so hot that our sweat-damp dresses stuck to the vinyl covers. It took him longer than usual to change the tire. No one said anything until he eased the car back onto the *carretera militar* that circled the island in its tortuous route.

"There are no poisonous *serpientes* on our *isla*," my mother said in a tone that told us, this is a fact, nothing more need be said about the subject. And nothing was.

The poem is closer to my emotional memory of this incident; the prose is an extrapolation that began with the facts of the event. In both the poem and the prose, I wanted to get off the subject in order to throw a different slant on the truth of the subject.

In his extraordinary little book on the writing life, *The Triggering Town*, the poet Richard Hugo talks about writing "off the subject." The "town" that may trigger the poem will not be the final town in the poem, if there is a town left in it at all. In my own work I have often taken this process in a different direction and used my poems as triggers for my essays and fiction. For me, it's a mental shortcut, a bypassing of a few steps necessary for the creative impulse to kick in. It involves attaining a sort of out-of-body state for me. First I have to distance myself from the persona of the poem enough to be able to see myself as a character outside of me, the writer.

In the case of the sugar cane scene I vividly recall the family road trips around the island, the macho driving and the blowouts in the white-hot tropical heat. As an adult I can now imagine the tensions those little contretemps must have generated between my parents, and for my purposes, I have assigned rays of meaning to these ordinary events. In the poem I focused on the triad of mother–father–daughter and the sexual politics between the adults that will also affect the girl at the subconscious level. It is the mother lode, the hoard of the writer, these buried insights that surface during the making of the poem or story.

Sometimes, after I finish a poem, the poem continues to haunt me. "You are not finished with me," it whines, "give me a chance to explain myself." This was the case with "Invisible Me," which eventually formed the nucleus of the essay about language acquisition that follows it. It is the same in the other prose pieces that begin or end in a poem. Having exhausted the possibilities in one form, I then try to explore the character or event in another genre. "Tell all the Truth but tell it slant," said Emily Dickinson, and what choice did she, does any writer, have? A story can be told many times in different ways, and a different aspect of the truth will emerge. So I begin again. There were sugar cane fields, and trips in my father's Studebaker, and I was not allowed to suck the sweet juice of . . . oh, please I don't want to say it. Okay, it was the sweet juice of life. And there are no poisonous snakes on the island, and my mother wanted me to know that I did not have to fear the knowledge of good and evil. And to this day I experience the thrill of the forbidden when I eat the forbidden fruit, when I find a new slant for an old story.

it's like this

The discovery of any surprising likeness is one more clue

to the suspicion that there seems to be an order, however

deep and mysterious, in the universe.

—John Frederick Nims

OVER THE YEARS I've kept up my connections to Spanish through correspondence and conversations with my mother, who returned to the island twenty-five years ago and reinvented herself as an island *Puertorriqueña*. In writing to and about her I have discovered that we newcomers to America are morphers rather than assimilationists, at least those of us who cannot or will not melt into the American pot. We shift our shapes, learn new vocabularies, and move ourselves or our modes to a climate that better suits our skin or personality types. I stayed with English, she returned to Spanish, and we live, with our choice of mother tongue, very different lives.

Early on, I learned to travel and connect these parallel roads. The poem was my vehicle.

Where You Need to Go
(A visit home to Puerto Rico)

My life began here in this *pueblo*
now straining against its boundaries
and still confused about its identity:
Spanish village or tourist rest-stop,
with its centuries-old church

where pilgrims on their knees beg

a dark Madonna for a miracle,

then go to lunch at Burger King.

Here is the place

where I first wailed for life

in a pre-language understood by all

in the woman–house where I was born,

where absent men in military uniform

paraded on walls alongside calendars

and crosses; and telegrams were delivered

by frightened adolescent boys

who believed all coded words from Korea

were about death. But sometimes

they were just a "*Bueno, Mujer*,"

to the women who carried on

their blood duties on the home-front.

I know this place,

although I've been away most of my life.

I've never really recovered

from my plunge, that balmy February day,

into the unsteady hands

of the nearly blind midwife,

as she mumbled prayers in Latin

to the Holy Mother, who had Herself

been spared the anguish

this old woman witnessed all those years;

to the aroma of herbal teas

brewed for power in *la lucha*, and the haunting

of the strangely manic music

that accompanies both beginnings

and endings here. I absorbed it all
through my pores. It remains
with me still, as a vague urge
to reconnect.

Today, opening my eyes again
in my mother's house,
I know I will experience certain things
that come to me in dreams, and déjá vu,
and memory: the timeless tolling of bells,
because time must be marked for mortal days
in seconds and in measured intervals,
to remind them as they drink their morning *café*
that they will die; the rustling of palm fronds
against venetian blinds, kitchen sounds
from my childhood; and muffled words
I cannot quite decipher, spoken in a language
I now have to translate, like signs
in a foreign airport you recognize
as universal symbols, and soon
their true meaning will come to you. It must.
For this is the place where you decide
where you need to go.

los sueños and poetry

ONE YEAR I WAS HAVING disturbing dreams of highly confusing content. I was also having trouble writing poems. My mother sent me a book of dreams in Spanish to help me decipher the secrets that my unconscious mind was having a hard time communicating to my reluctant brain. The book fascinated me by its total disregard of scientific facts. It did not refer once to Freud or neuroscience. I loved its poetic approach to the nightly flights of our souls to a realm as substantive in their implications as that of *el mundo* of our daily lives. From these interpretations (which I in turn translated and in the process reinterpreted for myself), a metaphor for my life between cultures became poems.

Variations from the book of dreams in Spanish:

AGUA

Water in your dreams reveals that there is much you must still plumb from your secret depths before you can know yourself. Agua rises from the womb of *la tierra*. If you dream that you are diving or fishing, you are really seeking an answer from your own self. Are you exposed to the elements of *el mar*? Is the wind buffeting you and you fear falling in? You must take control of your life. The elements are not your enemies; the danger is your powerlessness in their face. If water is falling in the form of rain, it may portend a renaissance for your weary soul, yet beware, if you are blinded by the water, if it drives you to hide, then you are afraid of the baptism, the near drowning that is required to be truly alive.

FUEGO

If you dream of fire, a consuming *fuego*, you should not doubt that you are ready to give yourself over to passion. Beware. It is never a purifying flame that licks your body like a huge tongue, inflaming you, but does not turn you to ashes. The ancients called fire *el hijo del sol*, the son of the sun. He was a god with a *corazon fogoso*—a hungry, fiery entity. It was reckless lovers who prayed to *el hijo del sol*. A dream of fire may mean a threat to your heart. *Ardes de pasion*? What do you desire? Do you smell smoke in your dream? Try to awaken yourself if the dream seems too real, and check the house for signs of fire.

My mother's book of dreams, with its insistent thesis that life, both in its conscious and unconscious manifestations, is elemental and decipherable, led me back to the wellspring of my subconscious life, poetry: the poems and the dreams blended together into a workable reality. I saw that my dreams were ingredients from which to make gold in my alchemy laboratory, or they were magical condiments, the eye of toad, the scale of dragon, tossed into my witch's cauldron. Metaphor making is both science and magic, and it is my main means of surviving *la lucha*.★ If I can make the ordinary new through language, then I can see the world as interesting and full of potential for myself. This gives me a glimpse of a meaningful life after the *lucha* of today; I guess you could call it hope. And if I'm really an artist, my *virtu* may also result in something of value to a few others. On the other hand, if the day ever dawns when I cannot look for truth through language, if words will no longer yield beauty, then the darkness will surely swallow me.

La lucha literally translates to *the struggle*. As I heard it used idiomatically by my Puerto Rican relatives, it seems to mean not only the work of daily survival but also the gradual wearing down of the immigrants' constantly embattled psyche. Under such circumstances I found little room for the artist—what he or she could offer was not considered a primary need. So to me, surviving *la lucha* meant making writing necessary, in fact, vital, to my life.

The Need for Poetry

Comes upon you with the sweet urgency
of first love, a sudden need to enter
another consciousness, another self;
a longing to slip into the white embrace
of the blank page; to suspend
the arbitration of calendar and clock
in a short vivid dream, to explore
the yet unimagined life on the other side
of whatever in you stirs, struggles
and flies, and in a sublime instant
surrenders to the attenuation of desire
that is the making of a poem.

"You can find beauty in the world by looking through others' eyes."

three

writers begin in the words of others

fountain, feather

I WAS A SMALL CHILD in the late 1950s and
grandparents in a small *pueblo* in Puerto Rico, w
occasionally and without warning shut off wi
road construction and housing developmen
amazement, is that when my abuela announc
ed. They simply organized for a day with
order of business was going to th
Obviously a language obs
recently, when

36

the yielding world

pen, fountain, feather

WHEN I WAS A SMALL CHILD in the late 1950s and early 1960s we visited my grandparents in a small *pueblo* in Puerto Rico, where the water supply was occasionally and without warning shut off while progress was made on road construction and housing developments. What I now recall, in amazement, is that when my *abuela* announced, "*No hay agua hoy,*" no one panicked. They simply organized for a day without running water. The first order of business was going to the river to collect water in buckets.

Obviously a language-obsessed individual from the start, what I remembered recently, when my mother brought up the *cuento* of our first time at *las plumas*, is that the word for *pen* is the same in Spanish as the word for *fountain* and also for *feather*, and that the first time my mother told me that we were going to *las plumas* because there was no water, I was very young and very confused about the multiple meanings of words in the two languages I was concurrently acquiring.

Las plumas, I heard her say, and I understood, we need pens: *pluma*, pen. Were we going to write to the governor to send water? I ran to get my *abuelo*'s Parker fountain pen, which I had secretly tried out and thus knew it still had precious ink in it. I had a *pluma*, I could save the day. There was laughter at my miscomprehension, and I learned a new word for writing pen, *el bolígrafo*.

¡A las plumas! I heard again, and I remembered: *pluma* also means feather. I imagined we were going out to where birds dropped their feathers and collecting a bunch. But for what purpose? Maybe to use in a magic spell to bring back the water? Or to dip in ink and use as writing *plumas*?

Someone handed me my beach pail with Minnie Mouse painted on it. The adults each got the zinc buckets used for collecting rain water and watering the garden, and we filed out in a procession of Mami, Papi, *abuelo, abuela, tíos, tías, primos,* and *primas.* We met neighbors also emerging from their houses with buckets and pails and pans of all sorts. Some banged on them like drums, and we sang any songs we could think of during the long walk to *el campo,* into the deep countryside and then the river. I led my cousins and other children in a rendition of the song I could sing better than anyone, being more or less bilingual by this time:

> *Pollito,* chicken
>
> *Gallina,* hen
>
> *Lapiz,* pencil
>
> *Y pluma,* pen.

Then we arrived at one of the most magical spots I remember from those early days on the island: a rock-covered riverbank where crystalline water poured forth in streams from deep in the earth and formed dozens of small burbling pools; some even spouted up like tiny geysers.

¡Las plumas! We all removed our shoes as if we were stepping on sacred ground, and we knelt in front of the little streams, cupped our hands, and drank the cool water before filling our buckets with the life-giving *agua.* Then we walked home, sopping wet, full buckets swinging in a joyous, raucous parade. What besides a one-day supply of water had I brought home that day? An abiding memory of natural beauty and freedom and joy.

As I sit here at my desk, hundreds of miles and decades away from a place that no longer exists except in my imagination (a road runs over the diminished river), holding my *pluma* in my hand, I watch the blank page waiting for the right words. I imagine a black feather dropping down and magically turning into words, or a fountain opening up before me:

pluma, pen

pluma, feather

pluma, flowing fountain.

I allow myself to recall the cool water running through my fingers on that hot afternoon of my childhood like a message from a deep place; to hear the music of buckets being filled and the laughter of barefoot people celebrating an unscheduled holiday. There is so much I cannot name in this scene that has stayed with me. It is my self-assigned task to make my *pluma* do the work of giving shape and sound to the unnamable things that have become a part of me. I know this: on that day I dug my toes into the soft sandy mud around *las plumas* and laughed and understood the pure joy of being exactly where I wanted to be. Who was I then? Not the wielder of the pen, not the writer who shapes her life in black ink. But it was on the day of *las plumas* that I gained an inkling about how the world yields and yields like a fountain, and perhaps it was then that I began to understand that when I capture a moment in words flowing from my little *pluma*, I am once again bringing up a secret from the deep in the cup of my hand.

Living in Spanish

How quick she was with the pun
or turn of phrase, rolling out her Spanish commands
at us all day; how she savored each word
on her tongue, even reading aloud
the labels of the bodega-bought
groceries, licking her lips over the *azucar*
en los dulces de chocolate, her favorite treat;
she'd even purse her lips, tasting the salty-codness
in the *bacalao* destined to be *guisado*
and served with the sweet ripe *platanos*.

And how she relished the thin romance novels
from Spain, whose titles she had me memorize
so I could get her the latest one at Schwartz's drugstore
as soon as they were set out on a rack like a carousel,
each turn a still life of beautiful lovers
precipitously posed in a near-kiss.

And how she shrank into her big winter coat
when we left the safety of her language refuge,
becoming a darker, smaller figure, and more foreign,
the farther she got from the four walls
she'd fortified with books and letters from *la isla*,
and long playing records of love ballads by Daniel Santos
and Felipe Rodriguez; our apartment, a microcosm
of the one place where she felt strong and fully alive,
a woman of many words.

As a teenager, how I hated the double-talk
of "my mother says," and "my mother wants to know,"
and the volleys of hostile looks among strangers
when I failed to make either side understand quickly enough.
The burden of the child translator weighed heavy on me then,
and at times I made things hard on purpose—*No se como se dice*—
I would claim to have no idea what she was talking about,
nor of how to make sense of her requests
in English.

How I wish I had known then about the things she did without
rather than beg me for words. Too much time had to pass
before I recognized the losses she suffered
in those years of exile from her mother tongue,
when she must have kept her *espíritu* intact
by living each day word by word, in Spanish.

word hunger

IT CAN STRIKE ME ANYTIME, but it usually happens summers when I'm reunited with my mother in Puerto Rico. Not when we embrace, and she tells me I'm too thin, and gives me her blessing, "*Dios te bendiga, Hija,*" and I respond automatically, "*Gracias, Mami,*" and tell her she looks younger than ever. It doesn't happen over the much anticipated traditional dinner she has prepared for me and my husband, *arroz, habichuelas, pollo, platanos dulces,* followed by ultrasweet *café con leche* and a *budin,* a small high-density square of such deeply satisfying sweetness that I suspect (but never want to confirm) it contains an entire day's worth of calories for most moderately active adults. It may not even happen while we are discussing the family gossip, health problems, an uncle with diabetes, aunts getting on in age, the family curse of arthritis slowly but certainly descending over most of us in the immediate and extended maternal side of my family. Diabetes, arthritis—both have cognates in Spanish. The word hunger is at bay for now.

It usually accosts me when the conversation takes a turn, and enters a subject in Spanish that I live with only in English: politics, medical conditions that I have not encountered during my previous visits, the intricacies of topics such as cooking, house building or renovating, current events on the island, and many other areas of interest to her and my Spanish-only relatives. It is those awkward pauses in conversation that I now call my episodes of word hunger.

"*¿Que crees?*" someone will invite me to offer my opinion, and it strikes, word hunger. I search frantically through my brain files for an equivalent. Awkward moment of silence. *La Profesora* cannot cough up a simple answer to a simple question. Usually my mother, a great improvisational dancer, both on the dance floor and off, makes her move to rescue me, translating the unknown into a synonymous concept.

"Prices here for *una instalacion de unos altos* (an addition to the house) cost twice as much as in the U.S. *¿No creen?*"

Even with my desperate segues and my mother's conversational diversions, *La Profesora* loses face. I have an academic title—my area is creative writing and American literature at the University of Georgia, where even the Latina/o students in my classrooms usually prefer to speak in English; I rarely get to speak Spanish, even when I am asked to give readings to Latinos in the United States.

Occasionally, my mother lets me suffer through a word pang, at least for a minute or two, long enough to allow me to dig up *la palabra* from somewhere in the deep recesses of my brain, the parts still allotted to Spanish. So I can practice my Spanish. She lends me her *Buenhogar* magazines and *People* in Spanish so I can continue to acquire conversational vocabulary. And it works. I can discuss the lives of celebrities with some competence, and if the topic of setting up a buffet meal for twenty comes up, I can probably get a few words into the conversation. I usually spend the time at her house reading the books of contemporary Puerto Rican writers such as Rosario Ferre, Ana Lydia Vega, Carmen Lugo Filippi, and many others, and marveling at the beauty of my native tongue, especially when it sings at the hands of a talented wordsmith. I fall in love again with its cadences, and often feel like I am an onlooker at a banquet, kept out mainly because of happenstance and circumstance. I had to choose a tongue to serve me, and it had to be English. But I can dream in Spanish. *¿No creen?*

Yet there are times when the word hunger defeats me. It happens when I am trying to share with my mother or a relative or friend on the island something that is both complicated and serious, and all the words I can come up with date back to the last stages in my life when I was more Spanish than English speaking, my adolescence. I stopped acquiring working vocabularies in what became my second language then, became frozen in my native language around age fifteen. During my formative years we lived mainly in Paterson, New Jersey, and it was a tough city for PR kids who did not have a survival grasp of English, in TV gangster–affected street talk, preferably. I was also required to speak polite English at St. Joseph's Catholic School. Spanish became intrinsically related to our apartment interactions, and to visits at the homes of my relatives, where the children talked in English among themselves, while our parents discussed their *luchas* and travails in passionate Spanish. Mainly, in those years of rebellion, I used my Spanish with and against my mother. I had a good fighting vocabulary.

"*No soy tu prisionera. Todos mis amigos salen en dates con muchachos. No vivimos en tu isla. Estamos en America. Si, voy a usar* makeup. *Esta bien, no voy a usar* makeup, *por ahora. Necesito dinero, Mami.*"

I never had a reason to discuss paradigms, dichotomies or dialectics, pedagogy, or gender issues with my mother, unless it was the constant argument about what a *mujer* is, should be, and when it was appropriate to wear makeup (never), date boys (never), increase my allowance (that is for your father to decide). I could probably still defend myself well in these areas but no longer have to.

But I exaggerate a bit, as is my cultural privilege. Mother taught us how to write in Spanish so we could correspond with our grandparents, and because I was her interpreter, I learned how to deal with doctors, clerks, the U.S. Navy, the Red Cross, and the occasional lawyer. But I was her recording device and trained parrot; none of these matters were my causes, therefore I deleted the words or replaced them with more functional expressions to me as I distanced myself from my childhood roles.

Not long ago I was in a line at a gate in Hartsfield Airport, in Atlanta. An irate airline agent was dealing with angry passengers experiencing many delays and missed connections. In front of me a woman was desperately trying to find out why her flight to San Juan had been canceled. The attendant kept motioning her to move aside, telling her that he had requested a Spanish speaker to come talk to her. I normally do not get involved in airline disputes, as I have learned that airline personnel are quite capable of ignoring you until you have to declare temporary residence at the gate or wait for the next shift to take over and then ingratiate yourself to them. Travel is a humbling experience. But something in this woman's voice told me I needed to offer her my emergency Spanish. I asked her what the problem was. She told me she had to get home for her mother's funeral; she had been visiting her soon-to-be-deployed-to-Iraq son at Fort

Benning. Her mother had suddenly died of . . . I could not understand any more as she broke down crying. I explained the situation to the attendant, who actually showed a measured sympathetic response. I also made sure that the fidgety people behind me heard me explaining the woman's desperate situation. I said *hijo*, son, Iraq; I said mother, *madre*, *muerte*. There was a palpable shift in attitudes, and an almost imperceptible making of a bit of space for this suffering mother and daughter. Soon enough she was put on another airline's flight to the island. My Spanish had sufficed. This time.

But I have found myself featured in less flattering bilingual stories. Recently I was asked to give a talk at a Spanish-language academic conference. After all, I have various books, mostly about my experiences in two cultures, could I deliver a paper? After reading through the proposal, my heart sank. I had to admit that although I speak Spanish, I am not bilingual past a certain level. I would have had to ask my friend and translator of my books, Dr. Elena Olazagasti-Segovia, PhD in Spanish, University of Puerto Rico, to translate my paper, and then learn to pronounce academic words in Spanish (hard enough in English). I found the task not within my zone of Spanish-language comfort. It was hard to explain to my dominant-Spanish *colegas* in academia, many of whom feel no shame at all in speaking in heavily accented English and using translators for their work, that I am a Spanish-fluent, nonbilingual, English-dominant Latina. And I did not mention this thought to them—that until recently I too suffered from bilingualism-paradigm paralysis: "Either you is bilingual, Honey, or you ain't." *¿Como se dice* paradigm *en español*? I once heard two Latino academics practicing their paradigm "in" joke at a conference. One asks, "What is a paradigm?" The other answers, "Four nickels?"

A more significant family occasion that left me feeling word starved stemmed from my mother's decision to answer many difficult questions about my father's battle with depression and about the horrors I suspected he had experienced in the military, which I had only heard about in snatches and rumors. I needed the answers to these questions to help me understand and accept his early death in a car accident during one of his worst bouts with what she has always referred to as *la tristeza*. I had always respected my mother's prior reticence and had tried to piece together his story through other channels. Here was my chance to ask the source, the keeper of our shared memories of my childhood. And I knew what the questions were, but they had to be phrased exactly right. We were both emotional, and I could not run out of the room to find a dictionary, or turn to my laptop and google the translation. Not knowing what to say, and not knowing how to ask her, I was left stuck in my silence, and the moment passed, the window closed. I had felt the pangs, the spiritual hunger, but I had been unable to craft the right sentences out of the wordless pain. Now it would have to wait some more.

When I came home to my English-language life, I wrote everything out I needed to ask her, and laboriously translated it, committing the "right" words to memory, preparing my passionate Spanish, the one I will always need, for when the time comes again when I can use it.

Do I speak Spanish? Yes, I speak Spanish. I speak survival Spanish. I speak yearning Spanish, I speak nostalgic Spanish. I dream in Spanish, and it will have to suffice.

my mother's gift

MOST DAYS MAMI was *un huracan* of energy, keeping up with two small children, walking us to and from school, to catechism lessons, to Sunday mass; shopping at the bodega for the Goya beans and *gandules*, the Mahatma rice, the ripe *aguacates*, Libby's fruit juices—the foods that were a staple in her kitchen; she polished furniture and mopped linoleum floors to the songs of Felipe Rodriguez, Daniel Santos, El Gran Combo, a long-playing album invariably on the turntable. She seemed to be in perpetual motion, always getting ready for our father's homecomings from navy tours of duty—everything had to be perfect *para* Papi. In our Paterson, New Jersey, apartment, she created a tiny island, a refuge from noisy dangerous streets; and it took almost all of her energy to make a *casa* for us out of a walk-up in the core of a teeming American city. Her face often showed the strain.

Yet there were some hours in the evenings, or on Saturday mornings, when my mother was transformed. This happened when she picked up a book after all her work was done. While she was reading, Mami looked like a woman in love, a soft look on her face, eyes seductively lowered, a mysterious smile as if she had just learned a delicious secret. Wearing one of the colorful robes my father brought her from his navy tours of duty abroad, her feet tucked under her on the sofa, holding the little book in her hands, turning each page slowly as if reluctant to ever have it come to an end. Sometimes I would see my mother reach the final page, and without pause start the book from page one again.

At the time, I was not old enough to understand the power of books over a person's mind and body, but I could see that she was in another place, no longer just reclining on the sofa in our tiny New Jersey apartment. She had flown away, *volando bajito*, back to the *isla* of her childhood and early womanhood where words like *la familia*, *el hogar*, and later *el amor, la pasión, y la belleza* were whispered to her, and where her language was the only one allowed to be spoken. I now know that reading in her native tongue kept her strong during the early days when she felt isolated from all that she had known growing up in a family of eight children in a small Puerto Rican *pueblo*.

As I watched her being transported by a story, I would sometimes feel jealous. I wanted to go with her, to that place that made her smile, made her seem, not like the Mami who worried constantly about everything, but like the lovely young woman that she really was. As soon as I could, I started "borrowing" her novellas and reading them in secret. I firmly believed that she would not have approved, because the stories were about men and women in love—a subject I was not supposed to be initiated into for a few more years. I later learned I had underestimated her thinking in this matter.

Growing up in Puerto Rico, Mami had had a wider choice of books to read from her Papá's little collection. Her father was a carpenter with a poet's heart, a lover of music and literature, whose shelves included old copies of books people had given him over the years (sometimes as payment for his handy work). She had read his copy of *Leyendas Puertorriqueñas* collected by Cayetano Coll y Toste, and some of the classical works by island writers such as Lola Rodríguez de Tío and Eugenio María de Hostos. In her *exilio*, however, which is what she melodramatically called the years when my father, a career navy man, was assigned posts on the mainland, my mother was forced to buying the romance novels of Corin Tellado, the Danielle Steele of the Hispanic world at that time. These books were the only Spanish-language publications available in Paterson in those days, other than *La Prensa*, and some *revistas* the bodega sold. My mother bought everything she found in Spanish. I believe that it was her way of staying connected with her real identity as a strong, intelligent woman—the opposite of what she must have perceived she looked like as she tried to communicate in her halting English; she must have feared that others saw her as timid and perhaps even ignorant. Language is power. I learned this early from her—you are at your most powerful when you are communicating in the language you know best. For my mother it was, and still is, her mother tongue, Spanish; for me, it would be English.

Corin Tellado's thin *libritos* came out monthly and cost a quarter each. By the time I was in fourth grade I was assigned the task of going over to Schwarz's Drugstore to check the rotating display of foreign-language books to see if there was one Tellado title that Mami had not read. Since my mother believed (or rather, pretended to believe—she has confessed to me that she knew about my secret reading all along—she argued with my father, who did not approve, that it would help me keep my Spanish) that I did not read her *novelas*, she would have me memorize the covers and titles. This is also one of the ways I learned to read Spanish. Of course, all the covers featured couples gazing into each other's eyes or locked in an embrace. It was no easy task finding the detail that set one book apart from the other, so Mami would point out the color of the woman's hair in last month's Corin Tellado romance as *un poco más oscuro*, or her complexion *más blanquita* or *más trigueña*. The man usually received less attention (Mami was very conscious about offending my jealous father in word or deed even when he was on a ship in the middle of the ocean—the time when she did most of her reading). Occasionally she would say, *Mira, se parece un poco a tu Papi, ¿no?* if the male portrayed had my father's light skin and dark brown eyes, or perhaps a military bearing.

I now believe that it was my mother's loving attention to her books, the time she and I spent simply holding them and studying them like Ming vases or Monet sketches, looking intently at the cheap romance novels as if they were works of art, that taught me that books are treasure chests, or at least maps to buried gold.

So, I became a book junkie, too, my mother's habit passed on to me, not as a duty but as a pleasure. I too longed to enter *el jardín secreto*, to be seduced by words, but I read differently from my mother. Do I smile like a Puerto Rican Mona Lisa when I read? No. My daughter says I talk to myself, argue with the text, frown and make faces. Do I recline like a Roman goddess, my whole body given over to the *cuento* unfolding inside my head? *Tampoco*. I have to sit up because I am a compulsive notetaker and Post-it sticker.

Mami's reading habits are not what they used to be. I am constantly amazed at how far she has come from her *novelitas*. Now a seventy-seven-year-old widow, she has turned into a demanding and discriminating reader, indulging herself by devouring the entire output of one author (such as Isabel Allende and García Márquez) before moving on to another, a *mariposa* still tasting nectar from her *jardín secreto*, now in full bloom.

These days I am trying to give back to my mother what she gave me. In abundance. No longer one *librito* every month, a starvation diet for a reader with the voluptuous appetites of my mother. *Muchos libros. Libros grandes. Libros caros. Libros* for Christmas, *libros* for *el Año Nuevo. Libros para el Dia de las Madres.* Books for every occasion. I want her to have all the books she desires. I will buy them for her. Because I understand word hunger. Because she was the first person that I loved who loved books and held them in wonder, and because that's *quizás* why I became a writer.

"*Que siempre tengas todo lo que necesites,*" my mother wrote in a book she sent to me many years ago. It is a book of dreams in Spanish, one I had asked her to obtain for me, to use in writing my poems. Now I can tell her, Yes, Mami, I have all I need *y mucho más. Gracias.*

traveling with alice
in wonderland

... but, when the Rabbit actually *took a watch out of its waistcoat-pocket*, and looked at it, and then hurried on, Alice started to her feet, for it flashed across her mind that she had never before seen a rabbit with either a waistcoat-pocket, or a watch to take out of it, and burning with curiosity, she ran across the field after it, and was just in time to see it pop down a large rabbit-hole under the hedge.

In another moment down went Alice after it, never once considering how in the world she was to get out again.

I DID NOT GET PAST the first few paragraphs of *Alice's Adventures in Wonderland* before my seven-year-old daughter Tanya fell asleep. We were both tired from packing for her first trip alone to visit her grandmother in Puerto Rico. Tanya was very excited about the trip, but also worried that she would miss us and her favorite things.

I knew that once she got there, my mother would keep her busy exploring her beautiful garden of hibiscus, roses, orchids, and her backyard full of fruit trees, and taking her around our beautiful island. Tanya would be busy practicing Spanish and having fun.

When Tanya arrived in San Juan, my mother called to say that she had had a good flight and that we would stay in touch by letters so that Tanya could practice writing in Spanish. We would talk by telephone only on Sundays unless there was a problem. So when I heard my mother's voice again on the telephone that night saying that Tanya wanted to talk to me, I was concerned.

"I just want to know what happened to Alice," Tanya said.

For a minute I did not know what she was talking about. Alice? Did Tanya have a friend named Alice that she was worried about?

"After she went down into the rabbit hole," Tanya added.

"Do you mean Alice in the book?" I asked.

Yes, Tanya had been asking her grandmother about the book with so much persistence that a phone call to find out what had happened to Alice seemed necessary.

I soon realized that the story of Alice's adventures was important to Tanya while she was in the middle of her own adventure. It was a way for us to stay in touch with home. But how to read her the story when she was so far away?

My husband and I came up with a solution: I would record my reading of the book on audio cassettes (this was long before CDs) and mail them to Tanya; that way she would hear my voice, and she could also participate in Alice's adventures—another little girl finding new and unexpected things every time she stepped outside: "And so it was indeed: she was now only ten inches high, and her face brightened up at the thought that she was now the right size for going through the little door into that lovely garden."

We have a picture of Tanya lying on my mother's big bed that summer, giant earphones over her head, a look of wonder on her face, listening to the story that to this day she still calls her favorite. Even now, as an adult, Tanya remembers that Alice was her imaginary friend that summer, and that she imagined herself exploring her grandmother's house and garden as did Alice in Wonderland, discovering all the new sights and making friends with the creatures.

It is through reading that I learned how to find wonder in the world, and, just as my mother passed her love of books and storytelling to me by her example, I believe that my daughter learned a similar lesson by traveling with the wonderful Alice.

first class back to the summer of love

SOMEONE SMASHES A CIGARETTE BUTT on the outside of my window ledge. I tap on the glass with my fingernails to let him/her of the blue-black nail polish know that there is a life being lived within these ancient hallowed walls of academia. He/she presses his/her nose to the glass trying to see in. I let down the blind against the humanity—oh, the humanity. I return to my fat folder of "Visions of America in the New Millennium," the essay assignment I have given my Multicultural American Literature class. After reading about life on the rez, in the barrio, the ghetto, China-town, about the Japanese internment, the Black Power movement, the Chicano renaissance, the Puerto Rican diaspora, I asked them to give shape to their personal vision of America and write a brief history of their time and how their experiences shaped their individual American identity.

> I grew up in a suburb of Atlanta. Life was not always easy. My mother sat around watching reruns of *This Old House* and my father was married to his job at CNN, at least that's what my mother said about him. I hardly ever saw him. On weekends my mother shopped at Lenox Square, or took long walks at the Botanical Gardens, while my father did his second job, as he called it; he was a slave to "lawn maintenance." My vision of America may be different from that of the African Americans, the Native Americans, the Mexican Americans, and the Lesbians and Gays in your class, Professor Cofer, but that doesn't mean that I have not been oppressed. In high school I was the lonely bookworm. . . .

I put that one down and pick at random from the pile.

All through high school I kept a secret. I lived alone. Both my parents were sent to prison for selling drugs, and my grandmother got custody of me. But one day she just up and left for her sister's in Alabama. The message on my cell phone said "You a big girl now, Shakilla, I had two babies when I was your age. You can take care of yourself. Check comes every month and food stamps; you know how to sign my name. Too old for this. Going home to Alabama to die in peace." She left some numbers where I could call other kin I never met. Never used them. Got this Hope Scholarship all on my own. My vision of America in the new millennium is that you still look out for yourself; nobody's going to get your back. I'm going to be a lawyer, make money, maybe get my folks out.

Another afternoon, I am at my desk, writing. I should be reading student papers. Instead, I'm trying to work on an essay I promised a fellow writer for an anthology she is editing. She has requested a meditation on class in America and how I overcame economic and social limitations to become a writer and a professor. The topic makes me a little bit dizzy. It's the travel malaise I sometimes experience when I try to enter that treacherous time-warping wormhole to the struggles in my past that now seem like either boastful (see how I have suffered more than you, my fellow Americans) or family gossip. I may just write a poem on the sepia hue and the warping on my office window, caused by generations of cigarette smoke. It's rather in-triguing to see the lovely faces of the young through my glass darkly. Now that the smokers have moved to the lawn of this neoclassical temple where Literature and Classics are housed, I have turned my chair to face the win-dow to catch the last rays. The late afternoon sun has called the students to lie on the ground and warm their skin like iguanas in blue jeans. A lie-in for narcissism. They are protesting winter. They want to heat their blood for the Friday night mating dance. We have sex, we have piercings and tattoos, we have sex. What do they have, the office slaves still at their desks?

Turning back to face my blank sheet of paper, I notice a shadow moving across the opaque glass on my office door, someone politely let-ting me know that he is waiting for me to leave my office so he can dust, mop, empty the trash basket. If I decide to stay until midnight, he will have to either await my pleasure or come back early in the morning on a weekend to pick up after me.

"No, Josh," I say to Josh #1. "I said I *lived through* the Woodstock era. I said it changed my life, as it did many others of my generation. I had friends, a little older than I, who went to Woodstock." (Yes, I say to myself, it is possible to be a little older than I am, Class. Hard for people born in the '80s to believe that I was not in a soup line during the Great Depression.)

Josh #1 speaks the name of the place reverently. Woodstock. He sits to my right, absorbing what's left of my 1960s-era aura. He stares at me as if beneath my disguise of a middle-aged woman who should be addressed as Professor, there is perhaps a wild young thing once called by the name of a flower or the title of a song (Professor Blossom? Professor Brown-Eyed Girl?), one whom he doesn't dare yet imagine dressed in gauzy see-through Indian garments, starry-eyed, dancing ecstatically at the sacred festival. Josh reads my poems for signs and clues of my alternate existence. He cannot believe I have not written about the most significant event in rock and roll history. I will only answer direct questions on the subject of the sixties (a decade I am covertly researching in order to be one step ahead of them), and only because it serves me as a pedagogical hook, a way to get their wandering attention fixed on an optical illusion while I inject poetry into their veins. It's also refreshing to be seen as the old hippie as opposed to the multicultural representative and expert on oppression, American style.

Josh #1 is being sponsored as a dreamer by his single-parent father, a lonely rocket scientist somewhere in Texas, an expert on photographing the surface of the moon and Mars, who adores his only child. I met the elder stargazer during parents' day for honors students, and I know that my idealistic Josh #1 is one of the lucky ones. He will be allowed to follow the wanderings of his imagination with the safety net of unqualified love always beneath him, a nice change from many of my other younger students, whose career goals were programmed in with their preschool alphabet lessons by their helicopter parents. Even my Josh #2 is in prelaw, an enthusiastic member of every major student organization. He is the best poet in my class, but I will not tell him that he is a natural-born writer unless he asks. He will get his law degree with an emphasis on minority issues. His mother is a prominent political figure and an activist, and so his entrée into the elite law firms and political life in Atlanta. I have not met this busy woman. I only know that my best poet, Josh #2, is doomed to succeed in following someone else's American vision.

"With your help I am going to find your friends at Woodstock, Professor Cofer, and post the pictures on my webpage. It will be a collage made up of group photos, each person digitally enhanced. My father says it can be done. I've found a high school yearbook picture of you in 1968 on the web, Professor Cofer! Can I put it up too?"

Ay, ay, ay, bendito. I will not tell them that even digitally enhanced neither Josh nor anyone who visits his psychedelic website will be able to really see who I was then. What they may expect to see may be their teacher in pupa stage, someone training them toward correct grammar and guiding them through the intricacies of their native language. If they could fit in my one-woman time machine and drop into my life in the late sixties, they would find themselves in the immigrant's limbo that was my reality. Back then, I did not know, could not realistically hope that I would become an American woman, much less a writer and teacher. Like many Puerto Ricans of their generation, my parents were "trying out" America. As U.S. citizens, we have the option to be undecided as to what we will be: Puerto Ricans, or Puerto Rican Americans.

Our future was negotiated at the kitchen table. Any day my parents could declare that they'd had enough of *la lucha* in the cold, foreign city, and go back to their familiar hardships in Puerto Rico. No, I don't think my students would recognize the insecure girl I was then. I am so assertive in the classroom (perhaps as a result of my deeply ingrained fear of being outed as an impostor), that they cannot possibly imagine I was once the silent student in the back of the room. By making myself invisible I felt safe from the humiliation I had witnessed and experienced over broken English. I chose not to volunteer to speak until I had the necessary number of words in English in my arsenal, until I shed my fear of sounding dumb because of my thick accent and my stumbling over difficult sounds. I was the unobtrusive sponge on the bottom of the ocean, taking it all in, waiting until I felt adequate in volume and weight, until I had depth.

I touch Josh's arm lightly to let him know I appreciate his attention to my potentially glamorous former being, but I will not let him derail the class discussion toward the date tattooed on his arm and in his tender heart.

In my undergraduate creative writing class, I had assigned the students to research the decade that most interested them, and to place themselves or someone in their lives at a particular moment in time. It could be expressed in either prose or poetry. Many of them chose the sixties.

It is Josh #1's turn to present to the class.

> August 1969. The day the souls of 600,000 American youths were lifted to a higher plane. Jim Morrison's songs were my time-machine to this long ago moment that changed the history of rock and roll forever.

He leans toward me, heat seeking. I move my chair a bit further from his. Touching students even by accident is risky business in this era where an inappropriate facial expression or eye contact (or the lack of it) can be cause for an inquisition—although I can always fall back on cultural DNA as my defense.

Latinos are such touchy-feely people. Public displays of affection are so prevalent among us, that to others it must seem a genetic trait. But touching one another is a privilege we give ourselves in my culture. The right to give and expect affection and comfort on demand. At least this is the way it worked in my family and community. Never more so than in the year when my family's hopes for peace and prosperity in America began to give way to the dark months of senseless assassinations, riots, and a war that was dividing and subdividing us; there was dissent between the leaders and the people, parents and children, the races, men and women, gays and straights. Everyone had a fight to pick. My parents feared losing their tenuous claim to a life in this country, and they feared losing control over us. So they clung, passing their fears to us through words and touch, and we were all afraid together.

By 1968 Paterson was an urban disaster. Racial turmoil had been building in our city, and it peaked as the assassinations of Martin Luther King Jr. and then, incredibly, of Robert Kennedy took over the headlines, and we were at the throbbing epicenter of the crumbling structure: 45 Park Avenue, our ironic upper-class-sounding street address was located in the middle of one of those American neighborhoods that are like seawalls, encrusted with all that the waves wash onshore. We lived in a house originally owned by Italian immigrants, later by Jewish immigrants of the post–WWII years, and eventually subdivided into apartments to house the Puerto Ricans, Dominicans, African Americans, the ever-changing ethnic and racial multitudes. The danger of such a volatile mix came to a head during the riots in Newark and Trenton, which began to spill over to neighboring cities like Paterson.

While the middle-class offspring of America grew their hair long and shaggy, marched for peace, racial and gender equality, and the other privileges they believed belonged to all Americans, in my family we kept close to home and held our intense kitchen-table councils, where we children were told to walk straight to school and back home and where our civil liberties (which we didn't know we had) were curtailed further each time there was a drive-by shooting by rival gangs or looting reported in nearby businesses. No going out after dark, no bringing friends over—friends who might turn out to be false, troublemakers "casing the joint" to invade our home and violate us when Father was away. My mother embarrassed me by trying to hold my hand when we walked downtown to shop on Saturdays. Her fears went with us and came home with us. She kissed us and hugged us when we left for school in the morning as if we were going to be separated for years. My friends teased me about my clingy Puerto Rican mother and overprotective father, but I knew this was not normal behavior even for my relatives. Paranoia burrowed itself into our psyches that year, a parasite that would remain in our systems, feeding off of our insecurities, forever. It went South with us in our exodus from Paterson the year of the Summer of Love.

"Come on, Baby / light my fire," I quote from Josh's creative nonfiction piece. "Let us begin by discussing what line breaks do to the music of a poem. No, Josh, Josh is not plagiarizing Jim Morrison unless he publishes this poem. This is an exercise in form, remember? We will compose original poems for the next assignment. No, Josh, Morrison's lyrics do not belong to the people. They are copyrighted. I don't think Josh meant to accuse you of stealing, Josh. Can we get back to line breaks? I suggest we read this poem, or song if you will, as it appears on the page. We can discuss copyright laws later. Jennifer? Yes. Jennifer Kelly. Oh, Jennifer Reingold? I'm sorry. Jennifer, go ahead. Jennifer Kelly dropped the class? Okay. I'll make note of that. So, Jennifer, what effect does breaking "Light My Fire" into three-word lines have on us? You don't know Jim Morrison's music? Can we get Josh to post an answer to your question on our listserv?"

Sorry, my dear students nostalgic for a glamorized past. No. Woodstock made a minimal impression on me. The only person I knew who had actually been to Woodstock was an undersized boy everyone at St. Joseph's School in Paterson called Billy the Bud. It became his claim to fame. I heard him tell his tale three times and each one escalated in drama to the point where he claimed to have been airlifted in a helicopter after he tasted some of that "bad stuff, man—tainted LSD." Maybe it was true that the experience transformed him; his overdue secondary sex characteristics kicked in soon after. He grew a red beard, which got him suspended. He became a popular guy.

Woodstock meant little to my family and consequently to me.

We were not involved in popular culture; we were involved in *la lucha*. Our discussions started and ended in the kitchen of our Paterson, New Jersey, apartment. Our father brought the news from the world to us and translated it into Spanish for Mother. And the only news that interested them had to do with our finances, our personal safety, and my brother's and my education. All else was mainstream chatter, background noise.

By early 1969, the talk in the barrio was focused on the tensions and conflicts in the streets, schools, and factories. The unrest we saw in black-and-white on our TVs touched everyone's life in living color one way or another: businesses shut down in "dangerous" neighborhoods— the Italian brothers who owned the American grocery store on our street were particularly aloof to their Latino customers, and kept an unfriendly eye on us while we shopped. I no longer enjoyed the flirtatious banter they had carried on with me and other *muchachas* who were sent in for the odd item (our parents bought their soul food from the island at the bodega), such as a carton of L&M cigarettes for my mother, or a loaf of Wonder Bread, which I preferred over the hard, crusty loaves of *pan* my family ate. I had a crush on the nephew, who worked at the Italian brothers' store part time, and he had encouraged my interest, if only to practice his flirting skills. But the Year of Little Love in America, 1968, had created an atmosphere of suspicion among us that even I, at fifteen and trying hard just to be normal, just to be liked and fit in, could not ignore. When I felt eyes on me in the store, it wasn't an admirer's gaze. I was being watched as a potential troublemaker. This feeling of "looking suspicious" in stores, airports, and other public places has stayed with me. I learned that to certain people, I do not look innocent or trustworthy; that, in fact, as someone who works for the airlines explained to me, I bear a general resemblance to the composite sketch of the female terrorist all security personnel are trained to notice. In 1968, before the feminist movement made women equal to male criminals to discerning eyes, I must have fit the profile for the juvenile delinquent's girlfriend. I trace my social paranoia to that time: the year I stopped believing that it was the new reconfiguration of my body that was attracting the attention of men. It is with a dismaying sense of disappointment I still experience when I realize that I am being assessed and measured by a clerk in a store where I may be lingering too long in the aisle of designer bags that in her mind I surely cannot afford. The only benefit to this mercantile profiling is that I get to pay for my purchases faster than the trusted customers who must catch the eye of the scurrying cashier since they do not have an employee following them.

Another Friday afternoon and the halls are practically empty. We the academic elite observe the social Friday as well as any third-world country. Our business of leading the examined life for the sake of Western civilization ends early. I hear the custodian revving up the waxing machine. The smokers are scattering toward their tribal longhouses to light their fires. I catch a final glimpse of the late-day sun illuminating the columned facades and cupolaed rooftops on this university campus where I have found my intellectual habitat. I am safely ensconced within the ivory tower and I feel at home among my stacks of papers, my books, and my generation after generation of students. My future turned out to be a place I could not envision in my childhood or early youth, because no one in my family had attended college, much less imagined one of us making a living that did not involve *la lucha*. I believe I earned the price of every brick in my little turret. Yet I am always aware that I will have to work harder than the other members of this club to prove what I know and what I can do, mainly because I just don't look the part of the university professor. And when I step outside, I am once again the suspicious outsider. I put on "privilege" in the morning like a fine winter coat that protects me from inclement weather, but it is a borrowed garment, like those men's jackets and ties that some fine restaurants keep in case a customer walks in "inappropriately dressed." I have to walk outside in my own skin, which, to some people still represents, if not a threat, a bit of a challenge.

I hear the custodian moving around and around, doing his slow waltz with the floor waxer, down the hall toward my end of the building. I stuff my students' essays in my take-work-home book bag that will look pregnant (I refuse to buy a bigger one; to me it is like buying a larger size in clothes, an accommodation for more fat, more work, encouragement to fill the vacuum). The size of the bag's belly predicts my immediate future: a weekend of grading visions of America, and because I am an obsessive writer, of thinking about my own essay or poem, influenced, as it will inevitably be, by the comparison and contrast of my past to my present, of the visions of America I had, the ones I encounter, and the one I must constantly revise as I live.

The black man polishing the marble floors of this Hitchcockian hall of endless numbered doors nods solemnly at me as I tiptoe out, letting him know that I respect the lake effect of his work by my caution, my restraint. I will not be jocular nor falsely wish him a good weekend. His movements are a waltz back and forth in measured elegant swaying sweeps he makes his own silent dance. What does he think about? My brain does not allow me to rest even in repetitive movement. I take no pleasure in the Zen of ironing or the Tao of cooking. The only time I am still (more or less) is when I'm writing. But if this man has achieved tranquility in this, his solitary task done outside philosophy, how I envy him. He nods in my direction without smiling. I nod back at him, neither of us attempting to lock eyes in some pretense of mutual understanding. He is not looking at me anyway; it takes his full attention and weight to operate his heavy machine.

I have left the first few lines of a poem lying on my desk. I will start whatever I am writing as a poem, and I will follow it to my subject. Fact and fiction, myth, images, memories. The poem will always lead me to the truth. I have invented and reinvented myself in lines; in poetry I have created a refuge where I can distill my painful memories and make bittersweet liquor out of my most painful and/or joyful discoveries. It is the dissection of these images in straightforward prose that makes me a bit queasy. Memory is as malleable as any of the raw materials I use to make my art. Time changes the past's colors and textures, sometimes softening them like butter on a lens, and other times warping the reflections, turning remembered scenes into fun house images. Poetry allows me to defend my artifact, my made thing. The truth. I want to be able to claim with Virginia Woolf, "this is how I shape it."

In 1968 America went wild. Martin Luther King's assassination ignited riots in cities across the nation. Then Robert Kennedy's senseless murder left even my politically alienated family stunned. Father decided that we could not stay in Paterson since he was away several months each year on tours with the navy, and he feared for our safety. My parents spent a great dealt of time arguing about where we should move. My mother wanted us to return to her mother's house in Puerto Rico; Father did not want us to interrupt our education in English. He had come up with a "temporary" solution. We would move to Augusta, Georgia, for a year or two, until things calmed down in Paterson. His two brothers were stationed in Fort Gordon with the army and we had teenaged cousins there. My brother, then twelve, and I, fifteen, threw fits. We did not want to move away. Not that we loved our socially limited lives in Paterson, but Augusta sounded like a foreign land. And it was. We left our familiar war zone of the inner city just before the Summer of Love, and headed south toward a new American life we could not imagine.

In Georgia we had to explore a new landscape and we had to relearn spoken English with new inflections, acquaint ourselves with another set of customs and boundaries. We became aware that there are many Americas, and Georgia is as different an America from New Jersey as a peach is from a mango, and that saying we were from New Jersey and thus Yankees was at times a more socially awkward admission than explaining our ethnicity. Race in the South is a subtle system little understood by outsiders, and it was with a mixture of dismay and relief that I found myself neither in the center nor quite on the margins of turmoil and tensions of the civil rights era in the Deep South. There were not enough brown people here to make us players of any significance. I could stay silent and invisible until I knew if I wanted to remain in this America.

I am a cosmic distance from the New Jersey Puerto Rican girl who channeled her parents' fears and their all-consuming sense of being strangers in a strange land. I have lived in the Deep South most of my adult life with my family, and I have learned to see the beauty of the place where my husband and daughter feel most at home. I have learned how to navigate the complex nature of race and class relations by maneuvering through the labyrinth daily. Who and what I am to others changes by a simple act of leaving my office building on a traditional university campus where I enjoy all the rights and privileges and the attendant irritations of being a chaired professor in English. In English. Who would have believed it'd be possible in my Paterson days? If my parents had moved us back to the island in 1969 instead of to Augusta, would I have led a parallel life in Spanish? Maybe.

The difference is that those of us who achieve some measure of success out of class almost never "believe" our identities are real. I cannot ever simply relax and enjoy. I must keep acting like the scholarship kid, a way of being that allowed me to get the education I needed to be whom I could be and that still serves me to achieve my goals. I believe my malady is called the "impostor complex." I work at everything twice as long and hard as I need to. I make jokes in class about "losing my English" when I make a mistake, and I suffer agonies after a lecture or a reading, or even in a simple conversation when I think I have revealed my English-as-a-second-language ineptitudes: a wrong usage, failure to respond to cultural clues or to laugh at a joke because I am missing some crucial allusion. These can keep me awake some nights. Fighting phantoms is part of my parents' negative legacy, as is the feeling that I cannot rest. *La lucha* is forever, even now that I am living in the America *I* chose, and am doing what *I* want to do. I remind myself that I am like Don Quixote, dusting himself off after battling his windmills, reclaiming his dignity by proclaiming, "I know who I am, and who I may be if I choose."

we become the monkey girl

a prose poem*

I HAVE BEEN POSSESSED by Percilla, the Monkey Girl, and I am the medium by which you will become the Monkey Girl too. Stop reading this now if you do not want to be the wriggling thing covered in a coat of downy fur, extricated from Mother's womb on this spring day on the island of Puerto Rico. The midwife crosses herself and summons Father, who stares at me in horror and disgust, and will not touch me. And Mother screaming in the background, can you hear her? The neighbors do, and soon word gets around: a monster has been born to the Spaniard and his wife. The priest comes to sprinkle holy water in every room of our house, and says a prayer of exorcism over me, just in case I am the devil's spawn.

Stop reading this now if you don't want to hear Mother's anguished cries, *Dios mio*. Why did you not let this poor creature die? I feel you near me. You and I belong in Percilla's story now. We will be with her, as over the months, our luxuriant coat grows thicker, as the curls that should have crowned only our head, sprout over every inch of our body, and as our baby teeth pop through our tender gums in pairs—two of each. How we cry and beg to be comforted, our teething pain twice what any other child has suffered and everyone each day more afraid of the childlike thing with the sorrowful eyes, crawling, then walking on two sturdy legs, and growing. At some point, someone, perhaps a doctor, offers our parents words of hope: *en los estados unidos*, in America, there is a cure for every-thing. We remember the suffocating heat on the day when we are swad-dled in blankets and carried to the harbor in San Juan. There we board a ship and stay sequestered in a swaying cabin for days until it makes port in New York. Mother's ceaseless tears, we taste their saltiness. But never her sweet milk.

In the American city there are no answers for us, only more stares and whispers. Endless lines of the curious come to see us squirm and cry for attention like any child craving sustenance and comfort, yet to them we are nothing but a mockery of nature. The hunger of the crowds to lay eyes on his odd child gives Father an idea. On our return to the island, he makes certain we are fed well, and he commands Mother, who is pregnant with her fifth and last child and wild-eyed with apprehension, to oil and comb our pelt, as he calls it, to a gloss.

Everyone calls him a saint, a martyr, a model of resignation. He never touches us. We recall only the brush, the cold clippers, her trembling hands. We are never really held; we are passed from one to the other, kept like a wild creature at arm's length, felt, viewed, exposed: *Aquí tambien!* Mira, her hair grows everywhere! We remember the many pairs of prying eyes looking down at us at bath, at toilet, eating a banana—children like this scene the best, and feed us until we grow sick of the fruit—or are we imagining what will happen in the future? The carnival eyes, the chim-panzee partner in our sideshow act, who will be the banana eater, for we grow sick at the mere sight of the fruit that grows rampant on the island of our birth. We will not remember much of our native tongue, except for a few words. But this one comes easily to mind: *mona* in Spanish means fe-male monkey; it also means cute. And, on those occasions when we are taken out of the house, to be unveiled a little at a time by Father, no one can resist calling out *¡Mona, la niña mona, que mona!* At first the sun, warm on our head, is a comfort. Then the faces get closer and closer. Eyes. Many pairs of eyes. The sun drawn by our black hair burns us; we feel we will burst into flames. Terror and tears. Father saying, *Calmate*, Percilla, smile for the nice people, show them your pretty teeth. Soon we will again set sail for America, where the cool weather will be perfect for my well-insulated *niña mona*.

We will become one with the Monkey Girl on this journey. Ours will be the voices she hears when she takes her place in front of the eyes. Learn to love what refuses you, Percilla, and the world will be yours, *hija de nuestro Corazón*.

---

* Born in Bayamon, Puerto Rico, on April 26, 1911 to a normal couple, her Christian name was Percilla. She was afflicted with the so-called monkey-face form of hypertrichosis, which meant that, in addition to a full beard, and to her entire body being covered with coarse, dark hair, Percilla also had a second row of teeth. Given up for adoption by her father to Carl J. Lauther and his wife, owners of a carnival sideshow, Percilla was exhibited on tour from a very early age along with a chimpanzee partner named Joanna. She was billed as "The Little Hairy Girl." She is best known as "The Monkey Girl," the appellation the paying public preferred.

resources

the craft of writing and why it matters

an interview with judith ortiz cofer

What is the best advice you could give to aspiring writers?

The raw material in the best writing are the "moments of being" in your life, as well as the unforgettable characters you meet in life or in literature. It is the life-changing incident or event, the lessons you learned not in abstract terms but by experience, observation, reading, and passionate research that enrich your writing. Learn to observe and record everything that interests you; it will provide the images you need to make your poems and stories come alive.

What advice would you give to teachers of writing?

To have complete assurance you have to believe that what you are writing about matters. As a teacher of writing, you may have to expose yourself in expository writing. You may consider sharing some of your writing with your students, teaching them by your example that good writing allows you to discover who you are and who you may be become.

What do you hope for your students in teaching them writing?

That language is the greatest tool invented by humankind. We shape our identity by defining ourselves in words; we imagine our lives and make plans with it; we use it to explain, to defend; we use it to explore and to discover. We need it to survive. President Barack Obama has said that he became master of his destiny when he understood the power of words while he was still in college: "with the right words everything could change—South Africa, the lives of ghetto kids just a few miles away, my own tenuous place in the world."

Could you explain how your teaching of reading informs how you teach writing? How do you help students see themselves in what they read? How do you show them that writing is a form of dialogue with everything around them—the books they read, the people they know, etc.?

Reading brings us together. It makes us a community. Reading is both a private and a communal/sharing activity. Joseph Brodsky, the Russian poet who was persecuted and imprisoned for speaking the truth in his poems, defined the study of literature as the point of essential human connection. This connection is achieved when we read and communicate the ideas we acquire. Brodsky said: "A novel or a poem is not a monologue, but the conversation of a writer with a reader, a conversation that is very private, excluding all others. . . . And at the moment of this conversation a writer is equal to a reader, as well as the other way around. . . . This equality is the equality of consciousness. . . ." There is a place where we can all hear the same voice inside our heads, take a peek through the same partition into the human soul that a poem, a story, or an essay opens; perhaps even take the first step into a territory, a landscape of language, that we may all inhabit in an equality of consciousness. I knew at an early age that I needed books in my life. There were a few difficulties to overcome first, however. Chief among them was my insufficient hold, as a young child, on the English language. Before I could engage in the communal conversation, of partaking in the knowledge and the culture of this country or in reading with the others with whom I now hoped to share common ground, before I could go searching for my mentors' gardens, I had to learn the language of my adopted homeland. It was also a matter of survival. Beyond daily survival, language led me to the delights of reading, the discovery that literature is a spell against loneliness, a search for the other, a search for ourselves in the other. You are not alone when you are reading.

In pieces like "Underwater" and "A Life Boat," you talk about feeling invisible in school when you were young. Why is identity so important to learning?

Having an identity means having an awareness of who we are, where we belong, and also a sense that our lives have purpose and meaning. Without a clear idea of who we are, we cannot fully participate in our own story; we may become silent observers of life happening around us. For me, my sense of an individual identity began with my mastery of the language I needed for my cultural survival, English. Gaining knowledge through an education empowered me, allowing me to imagine a future for myself.

In several of the pieces in this book, "The Welcome Mat," for example, you describe yourself as an outsider to American culture; then in "Word Hunger" you explain that you are no longer quite at home with your native tongue. How does that betwixt and between inform who you are as a writer?

I believe that we all teeter, at various times in our lives, in between worlds. When we are children, we have a period of time when we have to learn to be adults; young adults must cross over into being middle-aged people, then toward becoming aging seniors. In between all our life passages we learn how to let go of certain things, find new ways, and acquire new vocabularies and new skills. So in a sense, we are all outsiders to a particular culture as we enter another. I do not see myself as being eternally alienated because of my ethnicity, but rather as a person changing and evolving and learning from each new situation. These new experiences are the material for writing. It would be a dull life if I stayed in one place, and I would run out of things to write about! This is all part of the story I will write while I live. And now, no longer the invisible child nor the teenage outsider, I face different challenges as I grow older and continue to examine my life in my work. The movement between the culture of family and that of the outside world is the basis of much of literature; although we go through similar experiences, each life is unique and every story adds to our human story, the story we all write.

[handwritten margin note: We: Student, Teacher, Principal — one of the same & yet, even I'm in transition]

Jonathan Currie has said that readers generally identify with the main character in a story because "we are more likely to sympathize with people when we have a lot of information about their inner lives, motivations, fears." Your frequent use of first-person narrative makes this act of identification even more likely. Could you explain some of your thinking behind this? Would you encourage teachers to start students writing in first person? Why or why not?

My writing is my journey toward self-discovery. I often use the first person in order to make myself stop and reflect about questions that are important to me—what do I think about this? how do I feel about that? Most people are in a hurry to get past the present moment. They want to keep moving, although most of the time they have only the vaguest idea of their ultimate destination. In the process of discovering our world through writing, we learn that it is the observation and reflection, the sights along the way, the wisdom gained, even the delays and unsavory characters we may encounter and the less than appealing rest stops, that are meaningful. It is a journey toward meaning that we embark on when we have included purpose in our plan; otherwise, we are like Alice in Wonderland, who at one point in her story found that the harder she ran the more she stayed in one place. An odyssey is what you have undertaken if, at the end, you have learned something about the world, human nature, and most important, yourself. The writer's journey is the one I know best, but anyone who leads a thoughtful life is on a journey, one in which she or he is the driver, not merely a passenger. The ultimate goal of writing: to impose some order on the random patterns, to give some meaning to our chaotic lives. Begin with your story; it is the ship that will take you on the trip of your life.

You've achieved great success in three very different genres: poetry, essays, and young adult literature. Many writers stick to one genre. Why is that not the case with you? What kinds of thinking inform your genre choices?

Much of my work focuses on the small dramas of ordinary people's lives at different stages of their lives. I want my books to be inhabited by a chorus of voices representing a variety of perspectives. I think that this plurality may be best expressed in a melding of genres present in much of my work. In trying various ways to tell my stories, my goal is to transcend the merely personal by exploring my subjects across genres, looking at things from different angles. I believe that as it is distilled through a poem, an event or idea may yield a different "truth" than when the same idea is pursued in an essay or a story. My books, whatever their genre, are a result of my seeking to hear the many voices representing the shifting landscapes of place and mind my characters inhabit, hoping to make the disparate elements blend and harmonize.

a different truth

How would you describe the process of beginning a piece, and what kinds of tools do you find yourself using most?

I begin by accepting failure as a real possibility, and then I put the first word down and start writing. If I sit down to face the blank page or screen expecting a masterpiece, I am going to get up disappointed, perhaps having accomplished nothing. I give myself a simple task to begin with—I make a list of images or words, or I read a poem or prose passage by a favorite author, one that I love and wish I had written. Then I may try to rewrite it until my fingers start feeling the words and my brain becomes engaged in the pleasure of making something that is uniquely mine. Writing, like painting or playing music, requires practice. You dip the brush in different hues until you find the perfect one to represent the colors you see in your mind; you play the scales until your hands are ready to have the notes come together in the melody you hear in your head. Words are the palette, the musical score. It's up to you to make them convey your vision.

What are your writing rituals?

At the point in my life when I understood that I needed to write for my life to feel complete I made a very difficult choice. My decision seemed a matter of survival; the elements involved were basic, immediate, necessary; and my method involved a simple, direct action taken by me, with consequences suffered only by me, and I hoped the rewards, if there were to be any, would be mine also. I started getting up at 5:00 A.M., before anyone else was awake. I was too busy during the day, and too tired at night. I knew I had to give up something to be an artist, and for me, it was that precious time before the sun rose. I learned to think of the two hours I had before my day began as the dark before the dawn. The dawn was whatever I managed to create that morning. Making something new with words became a reward in itself. I knew that my day would be better because I had done this one thing for myself. I wrote my first novel two pages a day for four years. Sometimes I kept both pages, often I threw one or both pages out, but eventually I had a book—a book that would not have existed if I had not begun my day with my writing ritual. I still get up early every day, and I write for at least two hours. My writing ritual is the discipline of sitting at my table every day as if my life depended on it—and it does.

judith ortiz cofer's writing tools for students and teachers

This book reflects the lessons I have learned as a writer. Although the craft of writing cannot be reduced to a formula, there are tools that writers use again and again; tools that help us generate ideas and make our writing speak the truth more strongly and clearly. The following writing tools may help you recognize your identity as a writer. Writing for you might not mean publishing books, but the act of writing helps us all become more aware of who we are and who we can be. Writing, in and of itself, is a useful tool for us all.

 ## become a camera.

Writers are aware that specific details carry the emotional truth of our experience. It is not just a matter of getting every detail exactly right (as it would be in a term paper or newspaper article); the writerly camera takes in the surroundings and interprets them. However, the first step in identifying the emotional weight of specific details is to become more aware of the specifics that define the details around us.

Find a place where you can unobtrusively observe a large number of people—a coffee shop, a bus, or train. Record as much as you can of what you see and hear. Imagine yourself as a video camera—recording sight and sound. Try to be as specific as possible by writing down the exact words people say and concrete details describing what the setting looks like and what people are wearing and doing.

✴ explore the importance of place.

As young teenagers my brother and I resisted the move from inner-city Paterson, New Jersey, to gorgeous Augusta, Georgia. All parental arguments were invalidated by my teenage anguish over leaving the familiar. More fresh air and green grass in Georgia? I enjoyed the fortifying city smells of exhaust and factory smoke. I liked cement, did not give a hoot about magnolias. I had seen the film *Gone with the Wind* and my only response had been—*at least Scarlett is not a blonde*.

No, I would not go gently due south.

My frustrated father packed the car with a final "It's not as if we're taking you to Mars." And we drove south through the night. My first sight as I leaned over the window, carsick, that first morning in Georgia was the Martian landscape of my future home—the red clay of Georgia.

In an early essay I described the shock of my Georgia landing:

> For me, it was a shock to the senses, like moving from one planet to another: where Paterson had concrete to walk on and gray skies, Georgia was red like Mars, and Augusta was green—exploding in colors in more gardens of azaleas and dogwood and magnolia trees—more vegetation than I thought was possible anywhere not tropical like Puerto Rico. People seemed to come in two basic colors: black and blond. And I could barely understand my teachers when they talked in a slowed-down version of English like one of those 78-speed recordings played at 33. (from "Advanced Biology," in *The Latin Deli*)

I am interested in the intersection of time, place, and identity in writing; that is, the moment when a place has been absorbed by the self to become the mind's identifiable homeplace. When does the imagination take root in a particular landscape? I am interested in the idea of locale as a trigger for imagination. In my work, I explore my obsessions by setting poems, essays, and stories in places I have known best: Puerto Rico; Paterson, New Jersey; and Georgia.

Many writers believe that their imaginations take root in the place where they learned the first important lessons of their lives; often this is where they first learned language and where they established their first relationships with parents, siblings, teachers, and schoolmates. I heard and learned my first words in Spanish in Puerto Rico, and although we moved to the United States while I was still young, I thought of myself as a Spanish-speaking Puerto Rican. The sights and sounds of the island were and are what come to my mind first when I think of home. Think of places that are important, to you, to someone you know, or to a group of people. Choose one place to write about. Is the place a house, a street, a restaurant, a country, a monument? Start by writing a description in sensory details. Use photographs, interview people about the place, look up the location in maps, books, on the Internet. What new understandings about this place can you uncover through research? Why is the place important? What do you or others love about the place? What do you or others hate? Often place is not the subject of our writing but part of the background; however, this practice of imagining place will push you to look beyond the physical details to the emotional significance of setting.

watch the movie of what happened.

I often begin writing by thinking about an emotion. Then, I remember specific moments when I felt that way and choose one, watching the past as a little movie from which I can pull images: the classroom, chalkboard, teacher, gym, from "Invisible Me," for example. These concrete details sharpen my emotional memory of that time, and in my planning notes for the poem I try to be as specific as possible in describing the details: what did the classroom look like? What details do I remember about the teacher? Although I didn't use those details in the poem, as I was planning they helped me think about what I was trying to communicate. This stage feels concrete, but memory always brings us beyond the literal description. Our memories are always colored by our emotions, both in the moment and in the moment we recall them.

Think of an emotion and remember specific moments from your past when you felt that way. Choose one moment and watch it in your mind's eye like a movie. Record what you did, what you saw, everything you remember, in as much detail as possible. Then, choosing the most powerful details, write an autobiographical poem or piece of prose.

examine your life as part of history.

What were you doing when . . . ? This is a question you hear often, especially about events that change things for a society, nation, or even the world. In "First Class Back to the Summer of Love," I reflect on my students' desire to attach a specific romantic stereotype of the 1960s to my identity and I explore the irony of the reality of my experience of that time compared to their perceptions of it. For my generation, the question asked often is What were you doing when President Kennedy was shot? There are words and names that call back memories for me: The Beatles, Woodstock, Martin Luther King Jr., Vietnam, and many others. I have written several stories and essays as an answer to these questions about where I was during historically significant events. By simply being alive at a particular moment in time, we are a part of history even when we are not directly involved in it. History affects all of us, in either minor or sometimes major ways. If you were in New York City on September 11, 2001, you had intimate knowledge of that terrible tragedy, more so than if you lived in California, Georgia, Paris, Tokyo, Rome, or any other place in the world. But in one way or another, this catastrophe has marked us all, and its scar is seen in the way we live now.

Writers use timelines as organizational tools. What events have shaped the world during your life or the life of a character you're writing about? Is it a war, a weather-related catastrophe such as a hurricane or earthquake? Or perhaps you or your character witnessed positive historical changes, such as the election of a favorite leader, or the passing of a law that made life better. Create a timeline of your life or your character's life to organize and generate memories of both the personal details and the major historical events. How did these larger events affect the individual you're writing about? Choose an event that had an impact and explore its influence. Write it cinematically, that is, in scenes, as if you were narrating a movie. This way the idea will be dramatized; by having your characters move, speak, and react to one another, you will be *showing* who they are and why they act as they do, rather than merely telling or explaining their motives and actions.

become a reader.

As a child, I changed schools many times because my father was a military man and we would move back to Puerto Rico when he was away for long periods of time. Books were my main companions. From watching my mother take so much comfort and pleasure in reading, I learned that you are never lonely when you have a book to keep you company. I believe that my life as a reader prepared me to become a writer. I absorbed storytelling technique as I read and enjoyed the stories, not knowing that each sentence was a lesson in how to use words to create pictures, and how each sentence took the story forward toward a satisfying conclusion.

I read to my daughter and encouraged her to read. Tanya eventually became a mathematician. (Lewis Carroll, who wrote *Alice in Wonderland*, was a mathematician, and he used math ideas in the story—did this have an effect on Tanya's imagination?) Knowing how much stories taught her, Tanya often asks her students to write stories based on math concepts they find difficult. So reading is useful in many ways. It helps explain us to ourselves, relate to others through shared experiences, and discover the world even as we are entertained. I read everything that catches my eye: newspapers, magazines, books on any subject that I think will be useful in my writing. Becoming a writer means that nothing is wasted: every bit of information that is interesting enough to collect will eventually become a part of a future poem or story.

What we writers read informs what we write. What have you read that mattered to you and why? Start to keep a journal reflecting on what you read that you especially love. Record long and short passages that are meaningful to you. Think about taking a story that you loved when you were younger and retelling it in your own words.

use poetry as a tool of revision.

The poetry-to-prose technique I use and teach is probably very similar to the intensive revision process that most experienced writers practice. I see it simply as a way to arrive dramatically at the point that serious writing begins for me: a respect for language that writing poetry demands. Not that prose doesn't require great discipline; it does. I believe, though, that it usually takes longer for the inexperienced prose writer to come to terms with the cutting and compression required of good writing; the poet must face that painful decision almost immediately. Stories and essays that pass through this process begin at a much higher level of thought and technical proficiency than prose written from scratch.

By moving from poetry to prose and then back to the poem, you can more easily identify your subject—that thing worth writing about. When you attempt to put your thoughts into the demanding form of a poem, you soon discover that if the underlying raw material (your ideas) isn't there, you can't produce a gem. Much like when certain conditions aren't present, carbon won't yield a diamond. Maintaining the connections inherent in your creative efforts rather than isolating each genre allows you to recognize genres as angles of light from the same source, transforming whatever they fall upon into something new. A writer can find the truth of a situation in her own poem, and by paraphrasing and expanding it, that poem can become focused prose, which has been extracted, purified, and polished from its core substance.

Writing is finally a matter of condensing, of miniaturizing; the quality you are after is concentration of language. Once grasped, it allows beginning writers to move toward the same results and then choose a genre: fiction, creative nonfiction, and/or poetry. I am simply saying that if there is truth, it will emerge in whatever shape chosen to mold it but with a slant. The moral is good writing is good writing is good writing. And that it begins with the pause of the artist before a blank canvas, the discipline of restraint that was best expressed by Richard Hugo when he advised the writer to "think small; if you have a large mind it will show itself."

write about others to learn about yourself.

"We Become the Monkey Girl" began as a class assignment for my weary students. It was the end of the spring semester and they were tired of working on their class projects. This final assignment asked them to write about someone completely unlike themselves. They were to research another way of living, another gender, race, ethnicity, or religion than their own, and then connect with that life creatively by writing a poem or story. Someone asked half in jest if this other being could be a circus freak or an alien. I said, "It's up to you." Then I went home and started looking for my own subject, as I often do in my classes, in order to be a writer, not just a teacher who talks about writing. I came across the story of Percilla the Monkey Girl under the subject line Sideshows and Circus Freaks. What caught my attention immediately was that she was born in Puerto Rico, just as I was. I was hooked by that one item, but what followed I can only call passionate research because I had not chosen a subject, but rather, a subject had chosen me. Her story is in my prose poem, although it is not completely told. Percilla was not simply a circus freak; she was a sensitive woman who suffered the humiliation of being given away to a circus and who performed in a sideshow, but she also loved and was loved, and lived a long, mostly fulfilling life among friends. For the poem, I chose to focus on her childhood because the effect I want to project is empathy. I want to enter the mind of someone totally unlike myself, and feel what she felt. I want my reader to become the monkey girl. I want my reader to understand another life from the inside out.

Here are some notes I took before I wrote the poem. Besides noting the facts, I am also looking for images I might use to create a memorable narrative; in other words, I have to take dry facts and add passion to the words. One example of "charging" diction is to say "we become the monkey girl" instead of "we must try to understand the girl born with a terrible disease." I tried to do this with every sentence in my prose poem.

She could dance and she could sing, and she was never lonely.

What fascinated me about Percilla was her ability not merely to survive her hard life but also to feel joy in the things she could do, such as dancing and singing. I learned from my research that

- The Lauthers bought her a chimpanzee named Joanna, who appeared with her in her act.

- As she grew up, it became clear that Percilla was a natural entertainer. She learned to dance by watching the carnival musical shows, and taught herself to sing.

- She had an exceptionally melodious voice, which is characteristic of many female sufferers of hypertrichosis.

The Alligator Boy loved the Monkey Girl just the way she was.

As I researched Percilla's life, I expected to read about a lonely, reclusive girl. I was delighted to discover that she found love and a soul mate in Emmit Bejano. I did not choose to include this story in my prose poem, because I wanted to focus mainly on an empathic connection between Percilla and you and me—*we* become the Monkey Girl. Adding another narrative would have lessened the impact by redirecting our attention. However, it was important for me to know all I could about Percilla, even if I did not use it all—knowing how she lived made her a real, whole person with a life that was not all tragic; rather, it mirrored all our lives in its moments of joy and fulfillment, as well as sadness. Some of the humanizing details that helped me imagine Percilla are:

- While the show was touring Cuba, an eccentric woman named Madame Obrea became interested in adopting Percilla, claiming she would pay for an operation that would correct Percilla's dental problem. But Percilla, then age seventeen, had fallen in love, and chose to stay with the carnival and marry Emmitt Bejano, the Alligator Boy, who had been in love with her for some time.

- Emmitt was afflicted with lamellar icthyosis and was completely covered, except for his face and hands, in scales. He lacked sweat glands and was able to perspire only through the skin around his eyes. This gave him serious vision problems, and he appeared to be weeping. Icthyosis is not dangerous or contagious at all, but people with this condition tend to leave a trail of scales wherever they go.

- Emmitt and Percilla married and lived a long, reasonably good life together.

- Emmitt and Percilla were billed as The World's Strangest Married Couple. They were a sideshow sensation and eventually ran their own profitable business.

- Percilla gave birth to a baby girl in the first year of their marriage, but the infant died of pneumonia at four months. She said many times in public that losing her child was the real tragedy of her life.

- The Bejanos retired in the 1950s and adopted a son.

- When in public, Percilla covered her beard with a scarf and told people that she was Hindu.

- During the last few years of her life, she shaved her beard every few days.

- Emmitt and Percilla's marriage lasted for 57 years.

It is obvious that I was engaged in passionate research in my quest to know about Percilla, the so-called Monkey Girl. She became more human to me with every fact I learned about her strange but ultimately not-so-tragic life. There is enough material in Percilla's life story for a novel, yet after several attempts at incorporating everything in a lyrical form, I asked myself what point I was trying to make: it was empathy. To me, the most direct form of expressing emotion and of building bridges between people is to tell a story as passionately as I can.

How do you get your ideas? I am often asked. The answer is that it is not so much "getting" an idea that starts me on a new poem, story, or an essay, but becoming passionate about a subject that has been assigned to me, that I have to learn about in order to do something I want to do, or most often, that I have to teach. Not all topics are equally interesting to me, but I have learned to find some aspect on almost any subject with which I can become fascinated.

Cszelaw Milosz said in his poem "Ars Poetica,"

The purpose of poetry is to remind us
how difficult it is to remain one person.

I believe that the purpose of good writing is the same: to open a small partition into your mind or into the mind of another. Whatever the subject, if I am writing honestly and passionately about it, you will know my mind. By reading and writing about what most matters to us, we pass it— what we have learned, what has shaped us into who we are—forward.

The foundation for all writing should be empathy and passion. The two realms of creative writing and research can meet when you write about a person who seems completely unlike yourself. By finding out as much as you can about this "other," reviewing your research with empathy, and writing in the first person, you move beyond thinking about another person's life in terms of events to thinking about the feelings behind those events. Find an unusual person to write about. Research that person's life and make a list of the items you want to emphasize in your writing (you will not be writing a full-length biography, so focus on what characteristics you most admire about your subject and concentrate on what drew you to him or her). How is this person's story about all of us? What did the world look like from this person's perspective? Then imagine becoming that person by including yourself in the story as a witness.

how i use judith ortiz cofer's work in the classroom

harvey "smokey" daniels

Author of *Literature Circles: Voice and Choice in Book Clubs and Reading Groups* and *Minilessons for Literature Circles*. Smokey has also coauthored *Subjects Matter: Every Teacher's Guide to Content-Area Reading*, the companion volume *Content-Area Writing: Every Teacher's Guide*, and *Best Practice: Today's Standards for Teaching and Learning in America's Schools*.

engaging with the work of judith ortiz cofer

The first time I hear Judith Ortiz Cofer read aloud, she walks quietly to the platform, slight and modest. She gently pulls the podium microphone down to her height. Then, in a quiet, unassuming voice, she begins. Within moments, we are flown to another place. Cofer sets us down in her childhood (and, of course, in our own), around the hemisphere, and in our deepest imagination. We stroll the aisles of a neighborhood bodega, envision the covers of her mother's romance novels, and feel our tongues betray us as we try to speak someone else's language. Like her, we feel alone and alien; we are becoming Others.

When she finishes, the room is hushed. But there's plenty of noise inside her listeners. We're moved and changed. I have a big lump in my throat. This writer, working in her second language (not that you'd know it), packs a literary wallop that few authors can match. The audience can't let her go.

This is literature, literature at its most powerful and public. This is the kind of writing I want to put in front of the students at Salazar School in my New Mexico hometown, and in the districts around the country where I teach as a guest.

When I was a student and a young teacher, the English teacher's job was to tell kids what the book meant. This was typically accomplished through a faux-interactive mechanism called a *lecture-discussion*: the teacher "pulled teeth" to get three or four students to answer leading questions, while the other twenty-six occupants of the room dozed. This was and is one of the most passive pedagogical structures ever devised. If you look in the dictionary for an antonym of *engagement*, it says "lecture-discussion."

Today, great teachers don't tell kids what a poem, story, or book means. Instead, they show students how to think deeply and interact sociably around text. While there are many structures and activities that can make this possible, Cofer's writing invites me to highlight two: *think-alouds*, which put the teacher on stage in a whole new way, and *written conversations*, in which small groups of students create sustained literary discussions.

thinking aloud about "living in spanish"

There is still room for us to "really teach" literature—to stand in front of the class and be an expert. But our proper job as experts is to *show students how proficient readers think*. We need to open up our heads (metaphorically, of course!) and model for our young readers how an experienced, curious, mature reader makes meaning in real time.

Proficient readers like us have an internal repertoire of cognitive strategies that we use to make sense of text. As veterans, we usually use these tools automatically and unconsciously. But when the text gets tougher (as in poetry), we start to manage our thinking more intentionally: we slow down, reread, make connections, notice details, visualize, determine what's important, ask questions, and so forth. For our students to prosper as lovers and critics of literature, we must unveil these unseen cognitive processes for them.

The mechanism of the think-aloud is simple: we read a passage aloud, stopping at prechosen spots to explain what is going on in our mind right then. In other words, we explicitly demonstrate the thinking process called *comprehension* (Daniels and Steineke 2011).

Poetry is the perfect genre for this kind of modeling lesson: poems are short, packed with craft, and require careful reading. All the fine poems collected in Cofer's *Lessons from a Writer's Life* work well for a think-aloud, but my kids have especially enjoyed "Living in Spanish." Among many other virtues, it has multiple stanzas, so I can model for the first few and let the kids practice with the others. Here's my lesson plan:

1. **Study the poem and prepare to teach it.** Well before class, read and savor "Living in Spanish" for yourself. Be alert for spots in the text where you notice your own thoughtful reactions: "Oh, this reminds me of my own family." "Wait, I don't understand this part—what's going on?" "I don't know that word, what am I going to do?" "I am really seeing this beautiful image in my mind." Be especially sure to mark any part where the text gets tougher and you have to adjust somehow—slow down your reading rate, wonder about a word definition, or go back and reread. Finally, select a few of these places (at least two per stanza) at which you will stop and share your thinking with kids.

2. **Hand out the poem and read it straight through.** Distribute a copy of the poem to each student and read the poem aloud, uninterrupted. This builds kids' familiarity with the text. (You'll think aloud during your second pass through the poem.)

3. **Explain the think-aloud.** *Today I am going to show you how I think when I am reading a poem. I am going to read "Living in Spanish" aloud to you again, but this time, whenever I come to a place where I am having a reaction and doing some thinking, I'm going to look up and tell you what's going on in my mind at that moment. And when I do that—when I "think aloud"—I want you to jot some quick notes on what I say. Don't try to get down every word, just a phrase or a label for what you're*

noticing. You write only when I am sharing my thinking, not when I'm reading the poem. Okay?

4. **Model.** Begin reading "Living in Spanish" aloud, following your plan to stop at certain spots and share your thinking. For me, this would sound something like the suggested language below. Yours will be different, because it will be your thinking about the poem. (The lines from the poem are in regular type; the moments when I look up at the students and vocalize my thinking are in italics.)

Living in Spanish

This title tells me a lot, doesn't it? Looks like this poem is going to be something about people who speak Spanish. I'll read on and see whether I'm right.

> How quick she was with the pun
>
> or turn of phrase, rolling out her Spanish commands
>
> at us all day; how she savored each word

I am wondering, who is she? Who is this poem about? She is commanding people, so maybe she is a boss or a mother . . . she is speaking in Spanish . . . and she seems to love words and puns. . . .

> on her tongue, even reading aloud
>
> the labels of the bodega-bought
>
> groceries,

I think she must be shopping. I know from reading a book called Bodega Dreams *that bodega is a term for a small store in a Latino community. Maybe it has the same root as "boutique"?*

> licking her lips over the *azucar*
>
> *en los dulces de chocolate*, her favorite treat;

Okay, sugar and sweet chocolate, I can translate that. Is she really tasting this stuff?

> she'd even purse her lips, tasting the salty-codness
>
> in the *bacalao* destined to be *guisado*

I'm lost now, is this fish? I have eaten an Italian fish called bacala. *I'll read on, maybe I won't need to understand all the words. . . .*

> and served with the sweet ripe *platanos.*

Ah, plantains, I knew that one. Okay, this woman sounds like a person with gusto, a word lover, somebody positive, even a sensual person. So far, I like her.

5. **Reflect.** After thinking aloud about the first stanza, stop reading and say: *Take a minute to review your notes. What did you notice me doing? What did you observe about my thinking?* Ask volunteers to share what they noticed about your reading and thinking process. Record these insights on a chart titled "How Experienced Readers Think." You'll probably get responses like: "You stopped and reacted," "You were making guesses," "You asked questions," "You tried to figure out words you didn't know," "You went back and reread," "You had lots of responses and opinions."

6. **Continue thinking aloud.** In the second stanza, I would stop and share how I am getting a richer picture of this person, who seems increasingly three-dimensional and lively. I'd note that I am getting introduced to the poem's narrator, who's running errands for the woman. In the third stanza I would highlight the dramatic turn in the poem; suddenly, this big personality I have been admiring is becoming small and weak as she leaves the safety of her home. Somewhere along the line I would stop and correct one of my earlier inferences: *Wait, back in the first stanza I thought she was shopping for groceries, but now I think she was sitting in her house, dictating a list.* After each stanza I would again ask the kids to notice and name my thinking "moves."

7. **Have students practice in pairs.** With two stanzas left, it is the kids' turn to think aloud. Follow the same procedure you used during the whole-class lesson. Group the students into pairs. Have them silently read the last two stanzas, marking some spots where they notice themselves thinking or reacting. Then ask them to take turns thinking aloud to each other. The one who lives furthest from school (or possesses some other random attribute) thinks aloud about stanza four first. His or her partner takes notes. Before they start, tell them: *This is not a reading conversation like we usually have. You are not supposed to get into a discussion of the poem right now. Think of your partner as an audience, and partners, just take your notes.*

8. **Circulate and coach.** Observe and offer help as kids think aloud for their partners. As kids are finishing up stanza four, tell them to change roles and think aloud about stanza five. It is not vital that every kid think aloud about every line. As you visit pairs, look for great examples or quotes that can become part of the whole-class share, coming up next.

9. **Reconvene the whole class.** Have students share their thinking about the poem together. They should have plenty to say. Only if they are completely stumped should you prod with questions: *So what do you think of the poem? Did you connect with the situation? What do you think was Judith Cofer's purpose in writing this? What lines really stood out for you? How did you handle the Spanish words?*

10. **Debrief the process.** Let kids talk about the experience. You might use prompts: *How did thinking aloud work for you when I was doing it? When you tried it yourselves? How did it feel to be talking about your thinking? Did this help you understand the poem better? How could you apply some of this process to your own reading in the future?*

Thinking aloud is not something you do once. You need to show kids over and over, using different genres, how smart readers make meaning. Want to really show kids something? Stand up and think aloud "cold"—using a text you have *not* read beforehand. That's really *teaching*.

written conversation about "who is the alien?"

Earlier, I was heaping abuse on lecture-discussion teaching. Let me continue. One of the problems with whole-class lessons is that with only one person talking at a time, there's little positive social pressure on anyone else to participate or even listen. It is too easy to hide or ride on the coattails of others.

Ideally, we want all kids in our classrooms to be fully tuned in and actively participating in any literature discussion. The obvious answer is small groups, where the net number of people speaking increases and the intimacy makes it harder to slack off or snooze. But then we worry that kids will get off topic or that the dominating "hogs" will eat up all the airtime and the shy "logs" won't say a word.

Written conversation engages everyone, balances airtime among group members, and allows kids to deepen their thinking through extended, silent discussion (Daniels and Steineke 2004). In what we might call "legalized note passing," kids sit in small groups and write short notes to one another about the piece of literature being studied. At teacher-signaled intervals, they pass their notes around the group, reading and writing responses to each other's thinking. After three or four of these two-minute writes, students shift into an out-loud conversation that's supported by all the notes they have just made.

With their richness and complexity, any of Cofer's works would provide perfect material for one of these "silent literature circles." My students have especially enjoyed talking about her story "Who Is the Alien?" Here's how I set up a written conversation in which all kids bear immediate and sustained responsibility for an extended discussion.

1. **Introduce the activity.** *Has everyone finished reading "Who Is the Alien?" Great. Today we are going to try a new kind of discussion called written conversation. Ready to try it?*

2. **Form groups.** *Pull your seats together to form a group of four.* Fives are okay, but only use threes in a pinch. *Each person please get a blank piece of paper ready to use. Put your initials in the upper left-hand margin.*

3. **Give rules.** *As we have this silent discussion, please follow these three rules:*

   • *Use your best handwriting, so everyone can read it.*

   • *Use all the time I give you for writing. Keep that pen moving.*

   • *Don't talk when passing. This is a silent activity.*

   You will probably need to reiterate these rules as you go along, especially with students who are new to written conversation. To help prevent off-topic excursions, tell kids you will be collecting the papers at the end.

4. **Initiate the writing.** *Ready? Okay. Now everybody write for two minutes. Write your thoughts, reactions, questions, or feelings about the story. What did it make you think of? What were the most memorable parts? Why do you think Judith Cofer wrote it? Wherever the story took you, that's what you should write about. Go ahead, and keep writing until I tell you to stop.* Keep time not by exact minutes and seconds but by walking and watching kids write. When most students have filled one third of a page, it is time to pass the papers.

5. **Announce the first pass.** *Pass your papers. Everybody got one? Decide which way the papers are going to go around your group and stick to it. Now what are you going to do? You read what your classmate wrote, and just beneath it, you answer. You can state your reaction, make a comment, ask questions, share a connection you've made, agree or disagree, or raise a whole new idea. Write for about two minutes. Just keep the conversation going!*
   Walk the room, looking over shoulders to get the timing right.

SAMPLE WRITTEN CONVERSATION

Cherie: I was really surprised that Judith Cofer watched *Star Trek* as a kid. She seemed like she was living in this whole Hispanic world, I guess I would have thought she'd be watching those Spanish soap operas or something. I liked it when she made a friend. When I first moved here I was hiding on the playground just like she was. My mother always argues with me about going on sleepovers too. I don't know what she thinks is going to happen. That was ridiculous all the work Arlene had to do, I would be out of there if it was me.

LaToya: Well, I can really identify with Arlene. I have to do a lot of helping out at my house, and sometimes I can't go out on the weekends because my mom needs me to watch the kids. And I can't just run away! I thought this was a good story because everybody has to go into strange situations sometimes. We had to go down south to meet this part of our family and it was so weird because everybody talked so different and ate weird food. They were nice though. But I felt like I was on another planet. Cherie, did you ever find a friend when you moved here? I would have been your friend, but I was going to Westwood then.

Billy: You funky homo sapiens are missing the whole point of the story. It's like Judith always thought she was the alien because she's a Puerto Rican, and then she goes to Arlene's house, this pretty white girl's house, and she finds out that white people can be aliens too, because she is White Trash. Look at page 31 if you don't believe me! It says she was put in her place and ignored. But this can happen to anybody. It's like you are an alien, I am an alien, we're all aliens. Sometimes we're alone, we just don't feel like we fit in. Especially you, Brenda.

Brenda: Very funny Mr. Bill. But I think you are right about the story. This must have been a pretty big deal in Judith Cofer's life to see that she was not the only person who felt different or was different or was treated badly. I think that's what she is saying at the end: "I put my life in perspective." She realized that she is not the poorest loneliest teenage girl in the world after all. She learned this big lesson from this. Knowing Arlene really changed her life. I think it is sort of sad and sweet that Judith keeps expecting to run into Arlene somewhere years later. It shows how much that friendship meant to her.

6. **Announce the second pass.** *Pass again, please.* You may need to reiterate the instructions about "no talking" while passing. *Now you have two entries to read, don't you? So I am going to give you a little extra time for the reading. And then you'll write for two more minutes. You may answer one person or the other, or respond to both at once. Just keep that conversation going.*

7. **Monitor writing and call third and fourth passes.** Remember kids will need a little more time because there is more to read with each exchange. Again, don't time this activity by actual minutes but by watching how kids are coming and calling *pass* only when most people have written at least several lines. Sometimes three passes is enough; monitor the energy level closely, and skip to step 8 if that seems right.

8. **Return papers to the originators.** You have to do this step to allow for odd-sized groups. If you have perfect groups of four, it will happen automatically. *Now everyone pass the papers around so that everyone gets back the paper that you began with. Now read the whole thing over and see the conversation that you started. You won't write an answer this time.*

9. **Shift to out-loud discussion.** As soon as kids are done reading, say: *Now please continue your conversation out loud for a few minutes. Use your writings however they help you.* At this point you can also add a more focused prompt if you wish, focusing on either personal response or literary analysis:

   - *At some time in our lives, most of us have felt like outsiders. Has that ever happened to you? Share those experiences with each other.*

   - *Did you ever have a special friend who was quite different from you? Or a friend that you lost in some way? Tell about that.*

   - *What does Cofer mean when she says that Arlene had been "made invisible"?*

   - *Do you think "calm acceptance" is really such a good attitude to take when you are suffering? Should Arlene have fought back or run away?*

   - *Why do you think Cofer wrote this story?*

Send kids back into their well-warmed-up groups to discuss these questions or continue out loud the discussion they began in writing.

10. **Share with the whole class.** Call everyone together for a short but valuable whole-class lesson. *Now let's see where your written conversations took you. Will each group please share one highlight, one thread of their discussion? Something you spent time on, something that sparked lively conversation, maybe something you argued about or laughed about. Or did you grapple with one of the questions I suggested? Who'd like to share?* Enjoy the conversation that ensues.

Student engagement with literature is something we can have in our classrooms if want it—and work for it. With fascinating literature like Judith Ortiz Cofer's, we are halfway to hooking the kids. But we also have to make the right arrangements. Think-alouds and written conversations are not exotic pedagogies, but they do require that we rethink our classroom role, recalculate time allocations, and nurture collaborative interactions. When we make these small adjustments, everything can change.

Works Cited

Daniels, Harvey, and Nancy Steineke. 2004. *Mini-Lessons for Literature* Circles. Portsmouth NH: Heinemann.

———. 2011. *Texts and Lessons for Content-Area Reading.* Portsmouth NH: Heinemann.

carol jago

Author of *Papers, Papers, Papers: An English Teacher's Survival Guide; With Rigor for All;* and *Classics in the Classroom: Judith Ortiz Cofer in the Classroom*

helping students see themselves as writers

Students ages 8 to 80 can benefit from Judith Ortiz Cofer's *Lessons from a Writer's Life.* I know I would have found this book an inspiration at many stages of my own writing life. But helping students learn these lessons demands artful teaching. Some odd quirk in our natures seems to require each of us to discover anew the power of language. To make this personal discovery, students need to write often, under many different circumstances, for a variety of audiences. The good news is that we now have research to support such instruction.

Writing to Read: Evidence for How Writing Can Improve Reading, a 2010 report by the Carnegie Foundation published by the Alliance for Excellent Education (Graham and Herbert 2010), provides statistical evidence supporting the use of writing as a tool for building reading comprehension. The study identifies three instructional practices that are entirely consistent with the literacy experiences Cofer describes.

- Have students write about what they read.
- Teach students the skills and writing processes that go into creating text.
- Increase how much students write.

The research makes clear that "teaching students how to write strengthens their comprehension, fluency, and word reading skills" (23) and that "increasing how much students write improves how well they read" (23). At last we have evidence supporting the kind of instruction many of us have long found effective for helping students lead literate lives. *Lessons from a Writer's Life* can be a vehicle for students making their personal journey to full literacy. So much more is at stake than test scores. We want students to discover the power of language to transform their lives.

try this with your students: begin by asking students to reflect on their own literacy practices

Mirroring the way Judith Ortiz Cofer opens her book by recalling experiences that shaped her development as a writer, ask students to complete a short survey of their own literacy practices. For some students it may be important that their responses remain private. Whether or not you collect students' answers is less important that creating the situation that invites them to explore their own experiences. Ask students to complete a three-column chart with the following headings. You could also simply dictate the questions to the class.

1. **Where do you write in your daily life?** at home? online? on your cell phone? in school? for work? Make a list of every time you wrote something down yesterday.

2. **To whom do you write?** Next to each of the pieces of writing you generated indicate the person or persons to whom you wrote.

3. **Why did you write this particular note, list, or assignment?** In the third column indicate the purpose for each piece of writing you generated. Did you write to convey a message, to remember something, to demonstrate what you know, to obtain something you wanted?

Asking students to identify their own daily, and often undervalued, use of writing helps them see the ubiquitous nature of literacy, how it is infused into their lives in ways that go far beyond performances for school. Have students talk with a partner about one of the times they wrote, explaining why they generated this piece and what effect the writing had on them and/or their partner-reader.

Then invite students to read "What I Know" (page viii). As they read, have students identify passages that struck them as interesting, surprising, or that raised questions in their minds, annotating the text in whatever manner feels most natural. In order to accommodate students' varied reading speeds, ask students when they complete the reading to write about one of the passages they underlined or one of the questions they raised. When you sense that everyone has had time to finish the reading and to ponder its message (or when you sense that students are restless and ready to move on), bring the class together to discuss how acquiring the power of language was a survival skill for Judith Ortiz Cofer. The following questions might help to stimulate the conversation, but I always begin by asking for student-generated questions. Often we never get to my questions at all!

- How did you interpret Cofer's statement that mastering the English language expanded her borders? What kinds of "borders" do you think the lack of language creates?

- Did you agree or disagree with Cofer when she states, "Boredom is nothing but mind hunger, and mindless entertainment is nothing but junk food"? How do you cope with boredom? Were any of the occasions for writing that you listed on your chart reactions or responses to boredom?

- Why do you think Judith Ortiz Cofer chose to conclude this passage with her poem "To Understand *El Azul*"? How are the ideas presented in the prose section revisited in the poem? What does the poem add to your understanding of Cofer's message?

If you are wondering whether research supports the kind of instruction I have described here, we have only to check once more with the Writing to Read study. The report makes clear that having students write as they read and after they read helps them understand the books we put before them. Whether or not you record students' annotations or freewriting in your grade book, the value of this instructional practice is demonstrable.

> Comprehending a text involves actively creating meaning by building relationships among ideas in text, and between the text and one's knowledge, beliefs, and experiences (Wittrock 1990). Having students write about a text should enhance reading comprehension because it affords greater opportunities to think about ideas in a text, requires them to organize and integrate those ideas into a coherent whole, fosters explicitness, facilitates reflection, encourages personal involvement with texts, and involves students transforming ideas into their own words (Applebee 1984; Emig 1977; Klein 1999; Smith 1988; Stotsky 1982). In short, writing about a text should enhance comprehension because it provides students with a tool for visibly and permanently recording, connecting, analyzing, personalizing, and manipulating key ideas in text. (Graham and Herbert 2010, 13)

The writing students generate around Judith Ortiz Cofer's "What I Know" need not end with informal personal responses. The text can also be used as a prompt for analytical writing. You might ask students to research what other writers—Eudora Welty, Annie Dillard, Toni Morrison, Jimmy Santiago Baca, or Maxine Hong Kingston, for example—have written about their writing life, and then have students compare one of these writer's experiences and insights with Cofer's.

If your lesson focus is the study of poetry with an emphasis on Judith Ortiz Cofer, you could have students read the poems in *Lessons from a Writer's Life* as well as poems from other volumes of her work and choose one they feel best echoes the themes of her essay "What I Know."

try this with your students: use judith ortiz cofer's poems as models

One of my favorite methods for helping students see themselves as writers is to ask them to write poems modeled after a master. Style imitation seems to free students from their belief that they can't write poetry as well as break them from many of the bad habits they've acquired when they try, for example, rhyme for the sake of rhyme, topics they know little about (rainbows and birds, for example), and unnecessarily high-flown language. Judith Ortiz Cofer's poems employ beautifully simple, concrete word choice and offer themes relevant to today's teenagers' lives.

Many of the poems in *Lessons from a Writer's Life* would work well for this assignment, but I particularly like "Invisible Me" (page 3) as a template for student poems. We borrow the original poem's syntactical structure, but all the "meat on the bone" is made up of original details and images. This kind of writing both opens up students' range of expression and helps them become more careful readers of poetry. The exercise dispels the notion that poets are intentionally obscure. Students begin to realize that some feelings require suggestion and imagery to convey and that they, too, have the power to spin their experience into poetry.

If you would like to link this lesson in style imitation to the study of a classic poem, you might have students read Emily Dickinson's poem "I'm nobody! Who are you?"

> I'm nobody! Who are you?
> Are you nobody, too?
> Then there's a pair of us—don't tell!
> They'd banish us, you know.
> How dreary to be somebody!
> How public, like a frog
> To tell your name the livelong day
> To an admiring bog!

After discussing the Dickinson poem, have students write for five minutes about a time when they felt invisible to those around them and how they reacted to these feelings. Then read Judith Ortiz Cofer's poem "Invisible Me." Questions to trigger discussion might include:

1. Why did the speaker in this poem feel invisible in the classroom?
2. Why did she want to be invisible on the playing field?
3. How did the speaker learn to deal with these feelings of invisibility?

Then offer students the following template to use for creating a poem modeled after Judith Ortiz Cofer's. I find it helps to have students use the original title for their own poems. If some wish to do otherwise, that is fine as well.

Invisible Me

As a child, _____

_____

_____

_____

On the playing field *(or some other location)* _____

_____

_____

_____

In time, _____

_____

_____

_____

Now I _____

_____

_____

_____

Borrowing Cofer's structure makes the challenge of writing an original poem less daunting. Because the student poems share a common theme, taken as a whole they create an instant collection. In terms of organizing the timing of this lesson, I have students begin writing their poems in class, and then ask them to revise and if possible type them up for homework. On the following day, students work on editing their poems. Because my plan is to post their finished poems on a bulletin board or to publish the collection in a booklet, there is good reason for correctness. Students who finish first I set to the task of proofreading, organizing the poems, creating a table of contents, and/or designing a cover for the booklet or a central image for the display. Students need real purposes for writing, real audiences for their work. The more I can bring authenticity to the act of revision and editing, the better results I get. Many students who would be satisfied with a passing grade are mortified to have their poem appear in public with errors. Again and again I have watched students look upon their work and see that it is good. They've joined what Frank Smith called "the Literacy Club."

These few pages barely scratch the surface of the instructional potential of Judith Ortiz Cofer's *Lessons from a Writer's Life*. I wish you and your students many delightful hours learning from her lessons and from one another.

Works Cited

Applebee, A. 1984. "Writing and Reasoning." *Review of Educational Research* 54: 577–96.

Emig, J. 1977. "Writing as a Mode of Learning." *College Composition and Communication* 28: 122–28.

Graham, S., and M. Herbert. 2010. *Writing to Read: Evidence for How Writing Can Improve Reading*. Washington, DC: Alliance for Excellent Education.

Klein, P. 1999. "Reopening Inquiry into Cognitive Processes in Writing to Learn." *Educational Psychology Review* 11: 203–70.

Smith, C. 1988. "Does It Help to Write About Your Reading?" *Journal of Reading* 31: 276–77.

Stotsky, S. 1982. "The Role of Writing in Developmental Reading." *Journal of Reading* 31: 320–40.

Wittrock, M. 1990. "Generative Processes of Comprehension." *Educational Psychologist* 24: 345–76.

penny kittle

Author of *Write Beside Them*, *The Greatest Catch*, *Public Teaching*, and *Inside Writing* and *My Quick Writes* (coauthored with Don Graves)

read. imagine. write.

I read *Lessons from a Writer's Life: Readings and Resources for Teachers and Students* in an afternoon, drinking in deeply the images, the voice, and the possibilities of each line. I filled two pages in my notebook with Judith's words—lines from which I will write for weeks. While reading I felt invited into her writer's workshop, where I could watch her work, learn from her process. There are lessons here for each of us trying to coach writers, and for each of us as we seek our own writing.

We have so much literature to share with students that I stuff each week in my classroom with all that I can—a poem a day, a short text—digging deeply into language, pig-piling these essays and stories, words and images on student desks. As I read *Lessons from a Writer's Life*, I found myself adding "Invisible Me" for quick writing next week, then "We Become the Monkey Girl: A Prose Poem," then "To Understand *El Azul*." There is much in this book to inspire any writer to seek more in his or her own writing: to pay attention to sounds, smells, people, and dialogue. Judith's poems and prose pieces offer mentor texts for an English classroom but also something even more important for my workshop—lessons in process. Because Judith's voice is strong, offering such a real and rich invitation, my students will listen.

LESSON ONE: "I begin by accepting failure as a real possibility, and then I put the first word down and start writing."

This assignment is critical in my work with students, and we will practice it again and again in our notebooks. I believe it was Don Murray who told me that notebooks are a place to hold all of the bad writing that is essential we do in order to find the good. The first word that comes to mind, put that down—no matter how trite or unformed that thinking is—write a cliché if you must, write "I don't know what to write"—just make letters into words and let your mind relax as your pen moves. Put your voice and all the chaos in your mind down: write easy, we'll revise later.

Failing with words? A guarantee. And it takes discipline to write when you know you'll likely cut those words later. No one likes to waste time. No one wants to accept failure: words that clang together, sentences that rabbit trail into rambling paragraphs, ideas that start and then peter out—no one wants to write in tangents and incomplete thoughts, but beautiful, smooth images like:

> . . . the cool kiss
>
> of a September morning in Georgia, the bell-shaped
>
> currents of air changing in the sky, the sad ghosts
>
> of smoke clinging to a cleared field, and the way
>
> days will taste different in your mouth each week
>
> of the season (xii)

come from this place. We must write badly to write well. Judith counsels, "put the first word down," and students will listen to her because her final products are so lovely. You can write your life, I say, and here's how to begin: with anything, with one word, as Judith Ortiz Cofer says. Just write.

LESSON TWO: "I give myself a simple task to begin with—I make a list of images or words. . . ."

Lists—yes—the easiest way in for writers at all levels with whom I work. Schools where I team-teach with colleagues in second, sixth, ninth, or twelfth grades respond well to this invitation. I ask students to imagine a person in a place and list what they see, hear, or smell. I model for them:

> I hear the clink of the spoon against the side of a ceramic cereal bowl—the quiet slurp of coffee—the pen poised above today's crossword—my mother begins her day at the worn table in the kitchen where the light creeps through blinds striping the table, her arms, her hair.

Writing lists of ideas does two important things for writers: it gives them the freedom to chase words without a destination; and it teaches them to pay attention to details, which is as good for writing as it is for living. We live in a moment, concentrating on one image, not trying to imagine the whole piece. Think small, write small, and allow the writing to lead you to something larger.

The next day we use Judith's advice again—a list—but this time using words or phrases. I ask students to get as close as possible to the language they hear in their head when they think, *What would she say about this*—?

These notebook exercises are experiments to see where (or if) we have more to say. My students find moments they want to put on paper, and then dig for details to make the image fly. Once I have a writer wanting to create, the rest of my teaching begins to soar.

LESSON THREE: "Writing, like painting or playing music, requires practice. You dip the brush in different hues until you find the perfect one to represent the colors you see in your mind."

I like word and sentence practice in notebooks, sometimes serious, sometimes playful. Today we had ten minutes of word work, bouncing nouns against unlikely verbs. We started with a place that matters, a place rich with memories: a backyard, a favorite camping spot, the locker room, the stage. I chose the tennis courts where I practiced daily for years. I modeled a list of nouns for my place: *racquet, ball, serving line, fence, calluses, sweat*. Then I asked students to choose a different place and the verbs that might inhabit it. I chose the kitchen: *chop, sauté, sift, bake, caramelize, whip*. Now let us cook together.

We created phrases by combining the two, seeking an original, just-right image for something we've experienced. *I whip my racquet back as the ball spins across the net*, I offer. *I chop my serve, sending it into the net*. I try a few in front of students, then turn them loose to paint with words, to dip their brushes into the ever-changing swirl of language. I feel Judith beside us.

LESSON FOUR: "Then I went home and started looking for my own subject, as I often do in my classes, in order to be a writer, not a teacher who talks about writing."

There are two things I love here. First, the idea of looking for a subject, the hunt. Students often believe that good writers are born with lots of ideas. Writing pieces fully formed, waiting to be transferred to the page. I work hard to dispel this myth. Judith is home looking for an idea, just like you and me. See her sifting through photographs? Looking out her window? Reading the newspaper? The process of finding her topic for "We Become the Monkey Girl" is one we'll practice: Read. Imagine. Write.

Second, Judith writes so she can be a writer *with* her students, "not a teacher who talks about writing." This is a core belief in my teaching, but it means exposing my failures as a writer to students, and that always makes me hesitate. This line reminds me of my classroom before and after I began writing *with* students. I remember the vivid difference. I can tell students to write with details, or I can stand before them, pen in hand, closing my eyes to picture something in my mind, finding words, rereading, revising, writing again—even just a few lines. My students are more willing to try when I wrestle with words and ideas and images, as Judith does, always seeking the best writing I can do.

LESSON FIVE: "The ultimate goal of writing: to impose some order on the random patterns, to give some meaning to our chaotic lives. Begin with your story: it is the ship that will take you on the trip of your life."

My student Nichole's eighteenth birthday brought a storm of chaos to her life. Her father messaged her at 12:01 A.M. on Facebook, anxious to know her after years of silence. She didn't know he lived in town; she didn't know how to respond; she couldn't concentrate in class or at home.

Judith says, story "is the ship that will take you on the trip of your life." I suggested that Nichole write her story to make sense of it. It was tangled and difficult—so many pieces to explain—but in creating a timeline of significant events and then writing moments, Nichole found her story. She wrestled with sentence structure and transitions, word choice and dialogue, of course, but she wrote with a purpose. She revised with an attention to detail that I could never elicit through an assignment, and she produced a story that eased her suffering as it improved her skills. Story has a power that Judith knows and writes about with such beauty. Our students must experience and know this power for themselves.

LESSON SIX: "Stop reading this now if you don't want to hear Mother's anguished cries, *Dios Mio.*"

In the closing section of this book Judith writes a prose poem based on the story of a baby born with black body hair and monkey-like features. I am struck by the voice in this piece. Judith addresses readers with the admonition, "stop reading this now if you don't want to hear." I will use this in class to help students understand the power of voice.

Of all the qualities of writing, voice has subtleties that are hard to define and model for students. I show them how voice can distance the reader from the subject or the author by using their textbooks. But voice can also be used to draw a reader near. The voice of the text can pull you so close to the experience that you feel the words rise up and thunder inside of you. *Let us try this*, I say. *Let us borrow Judith's voice and write what comes next.*

Stop reading this now, I write on the board before them, *if you are afraid of the smell of dying.* I stop. I tell my class that I didn't see that line coming. That I had an image of being in intensive care beside my father and tried to think of what exactly scared me. That might scare anyone. I turn back to the board. I reread the line, and continue: *Stop reading this now if you are afraid to find yourself beside your father when all of your time together has been used up. Stop reading this now if you can't imagine that end because I will take you there.* I turn back to the class. "I know what I want to write," I say, "now it is your turn. Take Judith's line and begin your own."

LESSON SEVEN, A MOST IMPORTANT LESSON: "I read a poem or prose passage by a favorite author, one that I love and wish I had written. Then I may try to rewrite it until my fingers start feeling the words and my brain becomes engaged in the pleasure of making something that is uniquely mine."

Pleasure in creation—now *that's* a reason to write. We definitely don't talk enough about pleasure when we teach writing. Students are often surprised at how daily work in notebooks leads to moments of freedom and ease with words. Serious expectations for an assignment can crowd out pleasure in the process of writing because those expectations bind us up. We feel unable to accomplish all a rubric or an assignment demands. Students need the unexpected pleasure of freewriting to discover what they have to say. This is a most important aim—one that should be in our Common Core Standards—for without joy, people will not willingly repeat an activity. If running did not offer pleasure, who would train for a marathon? I want a new standard: students will experience the *joy* of finding words for their hard-won truths of living. And if we don't experience, model, and lead them toward this joy with words, who will?

I know the pleasure of making something uniquely mine. I can capture my mother in her house now that my father is gone, crafting a new life through the stories she is writing for her grandchildren. I can touch what is mine alone through images, words, my voice and hers. Each student has that unique world to write from. We need ways to help them write it, for the pleasure *and* the challenge it provides, and because this writing eliminates "mind hunger": the boredom of writing for someone else's purposes and expectations, or writing about someone else's ideas. Yes, boring writing must be done in school at times, but it too often crowds out the experience of writing to feed the soul.

We want readers and writers for life. Judith Ortiz Cofer's *Lessons from a Writer's Life* convinces readers that writing can feed them, now and always.

also by judith ortiz cofer

If I Could Fly. Forthcoming (2011). New York: Farrar, Straus & Giroux. [Young adult novel]

¡A Bailar! Forthcoming (2011). Houston: Arte Público Press. [Bilingual children's book]

The Poet Upstairs. Forthcoming (2011). Houston: Arte Público Press. [Bilingual children's book]

A Love Story Beginning in Spanish. 2005. Athens: University of Georgia Press. [Poems]

Call Me Maria. 2004. Paperback edition, 2006. New York: Scholastic. [Young adult novel]

The Meaning of Consuelo. 2003. New York: Farrar, Strauss & Giroux. Paperback edition, 2005. Boston: Beacon. [Young adult novel]

Riding Low on the Streets of Gold: Latino Literature for Young Adults, editor. 2003. Houston: Arte Público Press.

Woman in Front of the Sun: On Becoming a Writer. 2000. Translated into Spanish by Elena Olazagasti-Segovia as *Mujer Frent al Sol* (2005). Athens: University of Georgia Press.

The Year of Our Revolution: Selected and New Prose and Poetry. 1998. Translated into Spanish by Elena Olazagasti-Segovia as *El año de nuestra Revolución* (2006). Houston: Piñata Books/Arte Público Press.

An Island Like You: Stories of the Barrio. 1995. New York: Scholastic. Translated into Spanish by Juan Elias Tovar Cros as *Una isla como tu: Historias del barrio* (Mexico City: Fondo de Cultura Economica, 1997). Translated into Italian by Pietro Deandrea as *Storie del barrio* (Milan: Arnoldo Mondadori, 1997). Translated into Dutch by Tineke Funhoff as *Verhalen uit de Barrio* (Haarlem, The Netherlands: Gottmer, 1997).

Reaching for the Mainland and Selected New Poems. 1995. Tempe, AZ: Bilingual Review.

The Latin Deli: Prose and Poetry. 1993. Translated into Spanish by Elena Olazagasti-Segovia as *El deli latino: Prosa y poesía* (2006). Athens, GA: University of Georgia Press. Paperback edition published by W. W. Norton, 1995. [Prose and poems]

Silent Dancing: A Partial Remembrance of a Puerto Rican Childhood. 1990. Houston: Arte Público Press. Translated into Spanish by Elena Olazagasti-Segovia as *Bailando en silencio* and published by Vanderbilt University Press and Arte Público Press, 1997. [Essays and poems]

The Line of the Sun. 1989. Athens: University of Georgia Press. Translated into Spanish by Elena Olazagasti-Segovia and published by University of Puerto Rico Press, 1997. [Novel]

Reaching for the Mainland. 1988. Tempe, AZ: Bilingual Review. [Poems]

Terms of Survival. 1987. Houston: Arte Público. Reprint edition published by Bilingual Review, 2001–2002. [Poems]

Sleeping with One Eye Open: Women Writers and the Art of Survival, coedited with Marilyn Kallet. 1999. Athens: University of Georgia Press. [Essay collection]

acknowledgments

I am grateful to the editors of the anthologies and journals in which some of these essays and poems first appeared, some in different versions:

"But Tell It Slant: From Poetry to Prose and Back Again": Included in *Writing Creative Nonfiction*, edited by Carolyn Forché and Philip Gerard, pp. 8–13 (Cincinnati: Story Press, 2001).

"The Lesson of the Sugar Cane": From *The Latin Deli: Prose and Poetry* (New York and London: W. W. Norton, 1993).

"Out of the Darkness: Writing to Survive *La Lucha*": Published in *Water~Stone Review* 3(1) (Fall 2000): 65–79. (Commissioned as the second annual Meridel Le Sueur Essay by the editors.)

"Word Hunger": Published in *The Other Latin@*, edited by Blas Falconer and Lorraine Lopez (Tucson: University of Arizona Press, 2011).

"My Mother's Gift": Published in *Latina* 8 (9) (May 2006).

"Travels with Alice in Wonderland": *The Washington Post*, 23 July 2006, BW8.

"First Class Back to the Summer of Love": Published in *Angle of Vision: Women Writers on Their Poor and Working-Class Roots* (Ann Arbor: University of Michigan Press, 2009).

"We Become the Monkey Girl": Published in *Image* 56 (2007): 54–55.

Reprinted by permission from the University of Georgia Press:

"To Understand *El Azul*": From *A Love Story Beginning in Spanish: Poems by Judith Ortiz Cofer* (Athens: University of Georgia Press, 2005).

"Finding a Voice: The Language of Survival": From "A Theory of Chaos," in *A Love Story Beginning in Spanish: Poems by Judith Ortiz Cofer* (Athens: University of Georgia Press, 2005).

"Where You Need to Go": From *A Love Story Beginning in Spanish: Poems by Judith Ortiz Cofer* (Athens: University of Georgia Press, 2005).